DUKE ELLINGTON

GENIUS!
The Artist and the Process

DUKE ELLINGTON

by

Gene Brown

GENIUS!
The Artist and the Process

SILVER BURDETT PRESS

Created and produced by: Blackbirch Graphics, Inc.

Project Editor: Emily Easton
Designer: Cynthia Minichino
Cover Design: Leslie Bauman

Manufactured in The United States of America

10 9 8 7 6 5 4 3 2 1

Library of Congress Cataloging-in-Publication Data
Brown, Gene.
    Duke Ellington / by Gene Brown.
    (Genius!)
    Includes bibliographical references.
    Summary: A biography of the renowned pianist, composer, and band leader who, in his more than fifty-year career, left a deep impression on jazz and popular music.
        1. Ellington, Duke, 1899-1974—Juvenile literature.   2. Jazz musicians—United States—Biography—Juvenile literature.   [1. Ellington, Duke, 1899-1974.   2. Musicians.   3. Afro-Americans—Biography.]   I. Title.   II. Series: Genius! (Englewood Cliffs, N.J.)   ML3930.E44B78   1990   781.65'092—dc20 [B]
    ISBN 0-382-09906-0 (lib. bdg.)   90-30408
    ISBN 0-382-24034-0   CIP
                                                                                AC MN

(*Frontispiece*)
Duke Ellington helped legitimize jazz as a serious art form.

Contents

*Roaming through the jungle, the jungle
of "oohs" and "ahs," searching for a
more agreeable noise, I live a life of
primitivity with the mind of a child
and an unquenchable thirst
for sharps and flats.*
—Duke Ellington

CHAPTER 1

GETTING STARTED: *1899-1923*

When Duke Ellington died in 1974, ten thousand people crowded into the Cathedral of St. John the Divine in New York City to attend his funeral. Another 2,500, who could not get in, stood outside. The man they were honoring was more than just a famous American jazz piano player, bandleader, and composer. James Lincoln Collier, an expert on Ellington, called him "the most celebrated musician of his era." Collier wrote, "His name was known to hundreds of millions of people all over the world, and it is probable that the majority of people alive at the moment of his death, one way or another, knew something about his music."

Washington, D.C., at the turn of the century.

In a career spanning more than fifty years, Ellington left a deep impression on jazz and popular music. He created tonal colors—sounds that evoked images and feelings—and harmonies that other people didn't even know were possible. Ellington was the only major leader of a jazz orchestra who also composed most of the music he played. His ability to get his musicians to express his ideas while still giving them room for their own creativity may be unique in the history of music. He was also able to combine the earthiness of the blues with the more formal and structured musical forms of classical music. This helped to make the music world take jazz seriously.

Ellington's talent would be pushed along by many lucky breaks. As he noted when he wrote the story of his own life, many people helped him on the way to success. But he was also willing to take chances and make the most of his breaks. More importantly, he was not afraid to follow his creative instincts wherever they took him—no matter what other people said. There were times when things looked bleak, but he never quit. He spoke from experience when as an adult he said, "Life itself is one big, long soap opera."

Duke Ellington was born Edward Kennedy Ellington on April 29, 1899, in Washington, D.C. The city was segregated at the time of his birth. Blacks and whites went to different schools, sat in different sections of restaurants and theaters, and did not mix socially. Blacks were living in one or two well-defined areas or ghettos in most U.S. cities. In the District of Columbia, that area was the Northwest neighborhood.

Many black people had moved to Washington from the South because they had heard that they would have a better chance of making a living. Government jobs provided thousands with a decent income, which created a fairly large black middle class in the city. But there were also about twenty thousand blacks living in poverty in the District of Columbia. Many lived in slums behind the large houses of the middle-class blacks.

Edward Ellington began life modestly. His loving family gave him a good start. This was important for a black child born in the United States at the turn of the century because at the time society offered little if any support for black people.

The Ellingtons considered themselves middle class, which helped shape Edward's opinion of himself. His father, James Edward Ellington, came to Washington from North Carolina. "Uncle Ed" or "J.E.," as people often called him, first worked as a butler for a rich, white doctor. Edward's father eventually worked his way up the social scale, becoming a blueprint maker for the navy.

James Ellington thought of himself as a gentleman. He had a taste for the finer things in life and spent money as if he were rich. He thought it very important to know which fork to use at dinner and loved to make conversation, using fancy, flowery words. He passed this taste for elegance on to his son.

His father's attitude toward women was also a model for Edward's later behavior. Oozing charm, James would say to a woman, "Gee, you make that hat look pretty." "Pretty can only get prettier," was another of James's lines, "but beauty compounds itself." As an adult, Duke would pride himself on his seductive compliments to women.

Daisy Kennedy Ellington, Edward's mother, wanted respectability more than elegance. She was a religious woman who made sure her son went to church every Sunday. And her family connections encouraged her to think well of herself. Her father was a policeman who knew many important people in Washington.

Young Duke Ellington, at the age of four.

Edward's sister, Ruth, wasn't born until he was sixteen, so he was raised as an only child. He remembers being coddled and spoiled. His mother, especially, let him know that he was her "jewel," that he was "blessed." Her words left a strong impression. "Do I believe that I am blessed?" Duke was to write many years later. "Of course, I do!"

Edward told his mother that he would not let her down. He was going to be a success in life. A childhood pal had nicknamed him "Duke," perhaps because he was already beginning to talk and act as if he came from a wealthy, cultured, even royal background. It was a name that stayed with him for the rest of his life. "Your son," Edward announced to his mother one day, "is going to be the greatest, the grandest, the glorious Duke."

Duke Ellington's parents gave him one other important thing besides their love for him—their love of music. Both played the piano, and his father sang in a barbershop quartet. Duke started taking piano lessons when he was a child. His teacher's name, oddly enough, was Mrs. Clinkscales. But like many other young boys, he was attracted more to baseball on a nice spring day than the piano bench. He abandoned the piano for second base and center field.

As he moved into his late teen years, Duke returned to music and the piano. Although he took some lessons from a teacher named Henry Grant, for the most part his musical education was less formal. The piano players at the pool hall where he hung out with his friends were his best teachers. The pool hall was next to the Howard Theater, where most of the major black entertainers in America appeared. Some of them dropped by the pool hall to relax when they weren't on stage. Their presence drew the local musicians who wanted to learn from and be heard by the best.

Doc Perry and Louis Brown, two of the many pianists who could usually be found at the pool hall, were musicians who Duke credited as a big influence in his musical education. He especially liked their tolerance for different styles of playing. They had formal musical training, "but they also had a profound respect for the cats who played by ear," Duke later recalled, "and in spite of the fact that their techniques were as foreign to each other as Chinese, they lauded them, praised them, and there was the most wonderful exchange."

Young Ellington did not read music well, but in a sense this gave him an advantage. Since it was hard for him to read the music others had written, he composed his own. While working at a soda fountain at the Poodle Dog Cafe in Washington, Duke wrote his first tune, "Soda Fountain Rag." A rag is a song that is played in ragtime, a musical style that swept America at the turn of the century. Teenagers writing music then were likely to compose it in ragtime, just as teenagers today would probably write a rock tune.

Ragtime profoundly changed the beat, the rhythm, of popular music. Rags were at first written just for the piano, without words, and the beat was more complex than in the later music. The left hand played a steady beat, usually in 2/4 time (one-two, one-two), with a kind of pumping, almost marching rhythm. But the right hand, playing the melody, did something else. It played to a slightly different rhythm—often a beat ahead or a beat behind the left hand. The result was something musicians call "syncopation."

The important thing, of course, was not what musicians called it but how it sounded. The different rhythms gave ragtime an upbeat, jaunty sound. Rags made people want to tap their feet and get up and dance. The beat was ragged instead of smooth, hence the name, "ragtime." It was lively music; just the right sound for an America in which many people now lived fast-paced lives in big cities. The style became so popular that soon even classical music composers like Debussy and Stravinsky were using it in their work.

Ragtime music also changed the way people danced. Couples had always danced with about a foot of space between them, as in the waltz. Now people began to dance closer together. It was at this time that Vernon and Irene Castle, a song-and-dance team, introduced the foxtrot, which was danced to ragtime rhythms. When couples did the foxtrot they danced close together, almost embracing. The Castles were white, but James Reese Europe, a famous black band leader of the time, conducted the band that accompanied their dancing. (The most famous composer of piano rags, Scott Joplin, was also black.) When Europe died in 1919, *The New York Times* wrote: "Ragtime may be Negro music, but it is American Negro music, more alive than much other American music. . . ."

All across the country, people wanted to go out and dance. Dance halls sprung up everywhere. And they needed musicians. This situation was ideal for a young musician like Duke Ellington looking for work.

When the opportunity came, Duke was ready. By his late teenage years, he was working hard to make himself a good pianist. James P. Johnson was one of the best at the time, and Duke made up his mind to learn from him. Johnson played in a style called Harlem Stride. It was like ragtime, except that the steady beat made by the pianist's left hand was bouncier—the left hand seemed to stride, or walk, back and forth across the keys.

Duke got a piano roll of Johnson's most popular tune, "Carolina Shout." Piano rolls were rolls of paper that enabled special player pianos to reproduce a tune just the way the musician played it. The paper had holes cut in a pattern that controlled the action of a mechanism in the instrument. When the roll of paper was fed through the piano by someone pumping its pedals, the keys "played" even though nobody was touching them. Duke worked the pedals and watched the keys. It was like sitting next to James P. Johnson as he played. Soon Duke could play "Carolina Shout" himself on a regular piano. When he finally met Johnson at a Washington concert, the older musician was impressed by the young musician and encouraged him to keep working at his music.

Before long Duke was playing at parties and dances. "I only knew three or four numbers," he later recalled.

"I played them slow, fast, medium." One night he played for four hours straight until his fingers bled. It was hard work, but it was worth it. He was finding that he could make a living playing in public.

Duke's first big break came when he was seventeen. A society band needed a pianist for a dance, and Duke got the job. It paid seventy-five cents for an evening's work. Even then that was not much money, but it was a start. At the dance Duke used a splashy technique that he had learned from another pianist. He pulled his hands away from the keyboard briefly after playing each series of notes. It was a bit of showmanship that people noticed and that helped get him more work.

Duke often played one-night stands in cafes—wherever a pianist was needed for at least one evening. The working conditions in these places could be rough. Many cafes were dirty rooms located in cellars, with very little decoration. Customers would often drink too much and become rowdy, dangerously so at times. One night, in a place called Jack's, a fight broke out. At first, people were throwing whatever wasn't tied down, but then it got more serious. Shots rang out. Fortunately, Duke was able to dive under the bandstand and watch the fracas from a safe place.

Duke's solo piano playing was leading him nowhere. It wasn't until he began spending a lot of time with other young musicians that the threads of his fame began to weave together. Informal jam sessions where the musicians would play together eventually led to the formation of a small band. This group was to form the nucleus of the orchestra that would make Duke Ellington world famous.

One of the musicians in the group was an old friend, Otto "Toby" Hardwick. Toby and Duke were next-door neighbors who shared a passion for baseball.

James P. Johnson, one of Duke's early mentors, popularized a style called Harlem Stride that bridged jazz and ragtime.

Toby played the bass fiddle in the band (he later played the saxophone in the Ellington orchestra). The bass was big—bigger than Toby—and his father had to go along on the band dates so he could help his son carry it.

Before long the band was playing for money. Duke was a good businessman as well as a good musician. He knew that although there was a big demand for bands in the Washington area, there were many bands looking for work. How could he and his friends get their share of the available jobs? The group was not famous. Duke figured that most people looked in the phone book when they wanted to hire a band. What caught their eye was the size of each band's ad in the classified section. So he simply took out an ad that was at least as big as those placed by the other, more famous, bands. Sure enough, the phone started to ring with job offers.

Ellington also made some money on the side by offering to paint signs announcing a dance when one of his bands was hired to play for it. This visual artistic talent was a creative impulse that Ellington almost pursued. In high school, he won a poster contest sponsored by the National Association for the Advancement of Colored People (NAACP). He also won an art scholarship to Pratt Institute in New York City, but he turned it down. Even as a young adult he used his art skills, painting signs and working on scenery for a local theater. In later years he sometimes got the urge to return to painting. More than once on his travels with his band he bought art supplies, but he just never found much time to use them.

By his late teens, Ellington was supporting his parents from his music business at the cost of his formal education. He left high school before he graduated.

In 1918, Duke married his girlfriend Edna Thompson, whom he had known since childhood. Their son, Mercer, was born the next year. Duke Ellington, not yet twenty years old, was a man with many responsibilities.

In 1919, Ellington met Sonny Greer, a drummer who was already starting to play with noted musicians and who was later to play the drums in the Duke's orchestra. Greer, like Ellington, came from a home with strict values—but not so strict that Sonny couldn't learn all about rhythm by constantly banging on his mother's pots and pans. Duke and Sonny found they had much in common and became good friends.

Duke, Toby Hardwick, and Sonny Greer began to play together regularly and called themselves The Washingtonians. Soon it was the only group with which Ellington worked. They had a grand time, playing late into the night, smoking big cigars, and taking a drink or two. Elmer Snowden soon joined them on banjo, which was often used as a rhythm instrument in jazz bands in those days. Then they added Arthur Whetsol on trumpet. He had a sweet tone—and he was good at reading music.

Greer provided what seemed to be the first real chance for the group to make a splash in the music world. Sonny managed to get a job with Wilbur Sweatman, a prominent black bandleader of the time. The most important thing about the job was that it was in New York City—the place where you went if you really wanted to make it big. Sonny insisted that his pals Toby and Duke come along.

The first trip the boys made to New York was profitable for a while, but then the work ran out. They had to play pool for money. The time was not wasted, however. For Duke, it was a chance to get to hear and know some of the greatest pianists of the day. He became friends with the legendary Willie "the Lion" Smith and struck up an acquaintance with Fats Waller. He also spent more time with James P. Johnson, learning the Harlem Stride. Ellington even got to play at some of the cafes and parties where these masters of the keyboard were working. But the need to make a better living caused the young men to return to Washington to regroup.

They didn't stay home for very long, though. The next year Fats Waller came through town to play a date at a burlesque show at the Gaiety Theater. Duke invited him to his parents' home for some of his mother's fried chicken. Waller urged Ellington to return to New York since that's where the action was and where he would have to be if he wanted to play among the best.

A few weeks later, Waller called Duke about a job he had lined up in New York City for The Washingtonians. So in 1923, for the second time, Duke Ellington left his wife and child in Washington and headed north with his young friends. This time they would stay, and their success would match anything Ellington might ever have imagined.

An early record from Duke's days at the famous Cotton Club.

CHAPTER 2

THE NEW YORK SCENE: *1923-1927*

Sonny Greer and Toby Hardwick went north first. Duke followed a few days later. He rode in a parlor car and ate a fancy dinner on the train. "After all, I'm a big shot," he recalled thinking at the time. "I've got a job waiting for me in the big town." At Penn Station in New York he bypassed the subway and spent his last dollar on a taxi cab ride to Harlem. When he arrived, Sonny gave him the bad news—no job. Fats Waller had been a little too optimistic. The Washingtonians were far from home and broke.

    This was one of the many times in Ellington's career when luck would intervene. In Washington, Duke had played the piano at a theater for a singer named Ada

Smith. She was known as Bricktop because of her flaming red hair. Bricktop ran into Duke and the other musicians in New York and said she would try to get them a job where she was singing. Her boss was Barron Wilkins, a leading citizen of Harlem, and his nightclub, Barron's, was one of the area's most popular spots. It was a place where many famous show-business people dropped by. Thanks to Bricktop, the Washingtonians became the house band at Barron's.

Barely out of his teenage years, Duke had a lot to learn—and not just about nightclubs and entertainers. His youth had been spent in a secure black, middle-class community, where he had many friends and a loving family. But now, as an adult out in the world, his life would be more affected by the conditions faced by other black Americans. In 1923, those conditions could make life difficult.

Fats Waller, best known as a jazz pianist, also played the organ.

No black person reaching adulthood in the 1920s could have had any illusion about having equal rights with a white person. In the South lynchings were common. Jim Crow laws separated blacks from whites in all kinds of public activities. This was legal under the 1896 Supreme Court ruling that said segregation could continue. Woodrow Wilson, who became president in 1916, came from Virginia and approved of this practice. He even allowed segregation in federal office buildings.

Black Americans who served in the army during World War I were treated like second-class soldiers. They were given mostly kitchen work, and units were strictly segregated. There were few black officers, and blacks weren't permitted to even join the marines.

In the rural South, where most blacks lived, people were poor—many of them very poor. With little opportunity to better their lives, many blacks decided to pack up and move to northern cities where they had heard blacks were better treated. In the late teens, about the time of World War I, five hundred thousand blacks moved north.

It may have been better in the north, but it was far from perfect. Blacks found jobs, but they were mostly low-paying and menial. Few could get skilled work even if they had the skills. And northern whites had their own prejudices. Racial tension broke out into riots in several cities. In East St. Louis, Illinois, in 1917, about forty black people were killed in racial violence.

The Ku Klux Klan, formed in the South after the Civil War by whites who wanted to keep blacks "in their place," now experienced a revival—all over the country. Between 1920 and 1924, Klan membership grew from one hundred thousand to more than four million in twenty-seven states. This group was responsible for the killing of hundreds of blacks.

In response to these conditions, blacks had begun to organize to protect themselves against discrimination and to advance themselves economically. In 1909, when Duke Ellington was ten years old, blacks and whites formed the National Association for the Advancement of Colored People (NAACP). In 1910, the Urban League was formed to help blacks who had moved to the cities.

Although Harlem had many of the same racial problems that other places had, it also held more promise for blacks. Most northern neighborhoods were not segregated by law, but by custom they were either black or white. When Duke came to Harlem it was in the process of becoming a completely black area. Between 1920 and 1930, almost 120,000 whites left and just under 90,000 blacks moved in. Housing discrimination against blacks was breaking down by 1923 because they were becoming the majority in the Harlem neighborhood.

The people of Harlem had to scramble to make a living, but life was still rich in this city within a city. The cruelty of prejudice and the hard times forced people to stick together. Just as in other New York City neighborhoods where most of the people were immigrants from other countries, blacks in Harlem got together in churches, clubs, and fraternal groups to support one another.

For anybody who cared about music, art, or literature, Harlem vibrated with excitement. Poets and writers like Langston Hughes and Nella Larsen were reading their works somewhere in the neighborhood almost every night. Painters like Palmer Hayden and Aaron Douglas were depicting the strength and richness of black life. And the sound of blues and jazz floated through the streets. This great upsurge in black culture is now called "The Harlem Renaissance," but at the time, pianist and composer Fats Waller described what it was like even better in the title of one of his songs, "The Joint Is Jumping."

Exciting as it was, Duke and the others still had to take care of some basic needs before they could join the Renaissance.

Where, for example, would they live? A typical household in Harlem was made up of young adults without children since younger people were more likely than older people to move away from their homes in the South. These young people only needed small apartments, but most rentals in Harlem had five, six, or seven rooms. The problem was largely solved by the people who rented the large apartments renting out rooms to strangers. It helped the people that needed housing, and it gave the person who had the apartment a little extra cash. Ellington and the other Washingtonians found such a place to live in when they came to the city. Once he got settled in Harlem, Duke sent for Edna. Mercer stayed behind in the care of Duke's parents in Washington.

Strange as it may sound, the housing situation in Harlem also had a great influence on the development of black music. It was the custom for many people to throw a Saturday night "rent party" to help raise the money for the landlord. The person giving the party would put up signs telling where and when the party would be held. When the so-called guests arrived and paid their admission at the door, they could smell the fried fish, fried chicken, ribs, collard greens, and potato salad that awaited them inside. For the poorer people of Harlem who couldn't afford to go out to fancy clubs, it was a good place to go for entertainment, to hear the latest jokes, and to exchange social gossip. A piano player usually supplied the music for about one dollar and all he or she could eat and drink.

Some of the greatest musicians played at these affairs, including Fats Waller and Willie "the Lion" Smith.

Rent parties also gave musicians a chance to hear and influence each other. In fact, they often competed to see who was best. These competitions were called "cutting" contests. Similar contests were held at small nightclubs in the neighborhood. The activities at the rent parties and the nightclub sessions were Duke's final schooling. They also gave him a chance to start carving out a reputation.

Some of the music The Washingtonians played at Barron's was soft and sweet. People came to clubs to socialize, and they often wanted to be able to talk over the music. But the band's repertoire also reflected the style of music that was now taking hold in black communities and crossing over into white society—the blues and jazz.

The blues comes from black American folk music. It consists of eight or twelve bars (measures) of music in which the first stanza of the lyrics is repeated. Several notes of the scale are flattened—moved down a half-step—to give the music its "bluesy" sound. These flattened notes are called "blue notes."

But what the blues is really all about is feelings. It is based partly on the "hollers" that slave field hands used to shout to each other to ease the weariness and pain of their lives. The music is also similar to the old Negro spirituals, except that it leaves out the religion. The people who played and sang the blues were not ashamed to talk about their sadness, longings, lovers' fights, and struggles.

The blues was a lot different from the music that white America was used to hearing. The blues didn't focus on starry nights, soft moonlight, and sweet romance like other popular music. It told the truth about how people felt and lived. It didn't just paint nice pictures on the surface; instead it reached right down into a person's soul. Today's rock and soul music sprang from the blues.

The first blues record was Mamie Smith's *Crazy Blues,* which came out in 1920. But the greatest blues singer, Bessie Smith, started to record in 1923, just when The Washingtonians were getting their first big break. Mezz Mezzrow, a white jazz musician, said of her style: "That wasn't a voice she had, it was a flamethrower licking out across the room."

Ellington, Greer, and the other musicians, being young, black, and living in Harlem, were greatly influenced by this music. It was the music to which the working people in the neighborhood listened.

Jazz was also starting to change popular music. This, too, showed up in The Washingtonians's music. A mingling of the rhythms of ragtime with the soulful sound of the blues, jazz was a unique kind of music. The combination of instruments it used and the connection between the group and the soloist placed jazz in a different musical category. The first jazz bands were formed in the South, especially in New Orleans. Brass bands that played dance music had been popular in this area for some time. The melody in these bands was played by a front line of trumpet (or cornet), trombone, and clarinet. The rhythmic background came from a bass and a drum, although sometimes tubas, banjos, and guitars were also used for this purpose. Every piece had one or more soloists who would invent—or improvise—their own part as they went along. This offered individual musicians a great chance to be creative.

At first The Washingtonians were not very original. Their reputation was built on being in the right place at the right time. They were one of the first bands in the North to be playing the new style of music, but it was still the solo pianists like Fats Waller who were leading the way.

Leonard Harper, the man Duke rented a room from, was in show business and was to give Ellington his next break. Harper was producing a show for the Hollywood Club, downtown in New York's Times Square, an area that had become the entertainment capital of the country. He needed a band for the show, and it was only natural to hire The Washingtonians, whose pianist was living under his roof.

The Hollywood Club, like Barron's, was in a basement. Like many clubs at the time, it was owned by gangsters. It seated about 130 people, and it drew more big tippers than did the Harlem night spot. Here the patrons thought nothing of tearing a fifty dollar bill in half and tossing it at the waiters and musicians. The club was open all night, and the band usually did two shows: at midnight and 2 A.M. It was located in an area that would expose Ellington to some of the greatest names in show business who often dropped by after their own shows.

All clubs at this time had to find a way around a big problem: Their customers wanted to drink liquor, but federal law said that they couldn't. Since 1919 it had been illegal to sell hard liquor in the United States. In practice, however, it was probably broken more often than any other law in American history. During this period, which was called Prohibition, gangsters made a lot of money because they supplied places like the Hollywood Club with illegal liquor for their patrons.

The Hollywood Club was a place where many white people could hear The Washingtonians. This was important if the musicians were to break into the big time. It would mean better jobs and the chance to make records. It also meant a chance to appear on the radio. A local station occasionally broadcasted from the club.

Black musicians with a white audience was something new. In the nineteenth century, the music most whites heard was only indirectly influenced by black culture. In the minstrel shows, whites put on blackface and performed what they thought was black music and dances—sentimental and comical ballads and dance routines featuring strutting and jumping. But with the birth of the blues and jazz, whites, for the first time, were listening to real black music in large numbers. White people were hiring black musicians and bands to play at their dances. Black musicians were even starting to appear in major theaters, like New York City's Winter Garden.

Ellington now began to compose his own music to tap this new market. He wrote the music for a show called *Chocolate Kiddies*. Needing the money in a hurry, he wrote it in one night. Although the show didn't make Broadway, it did play for a while in Berlin, Germany. He also wrote the songs "Pretty Soft for You" and "Blind Man's Buff." His main aim was to sell a lot of sheet music—the music that people bought so they could play the tunes on their pianos.

During The Washingtonians' engagement at the Hollywood Club, the club's name was changed to the Kentucky Club. But the most important change that occurred in the four years that Ellington played there was in the sound and style of music that Duke and the group played. This new sound came from the new musicians who joined the band. Ellington, in composing music for the band, took full advantage of what these new musicians could do. He listened to them very closely and wrote music that featured what they did best—playing soft or hard, bluesy or lyrical, fast or slow. This was the first sign of his genius.

The Washingtonians didn't have a true bandleader. Elmer Snowden, the banjo player who had been handling the group's business matters, left and was replaced by guitarist Freddie Guy. Some suspect that Snowden was asked to leave for keeping some of the money that was supposed to go to the other musicians. In 1923, Arthur Whetsol decided to leave the band to go back to college.

James "Bubber" Miley, the trumpet player who took Whetsol's place, gave the band a sound all of its own. He was already known as a blues player and had played with singer Mamie Smith. Miley was famous for two things: playing with a mute and growling. The mute was made of metal and rubber—a toilet plunger, actually—that he placed in the opening where the sound came out. It muffled the trumpet's sound and changed its tone. By moving the rubber part in and out of the opening while he played, he could make a wah-wah sound. But the growling, also achieved with the mute, made his trumpet sound almost like a blues singer.

The group's music now took on a rougher sound that echoed the hot jazz popular in Chicago at the time. The Washingtonians knew when they hired Miley that the people who came to the Kentucky Club liked that kind of sound. "That was when we decided to forget all about the sweet music," Ellington later wrote. Now the band played the blues, with Bubber Miley's solos front and center.

Miley also molded the sound of the band through his ideas for song arrangements. An arrangement is the way tunes, originally composed on a piano, are written for each of the other instruments. Some play the melody, others supply the harmony. In a small band such as The Washingtonians no two instruments were likely to be playing exactly the same notes. A good arrangement would give the band—each musician playing his part but blending with the others—a unique and pleasing sound.

Miley also had an indirect role in bringing his sound to the trombone part of the band. The Washingtonians

The great blues singer, Bessie Smith, in 1925.

hired Miley's friend, Charlie "Plug" Irvis, a trombone player who also used a mute. But Irvis's mute was different from what other musicians were using. He had dropped and broken his mute but kept using what was left of it. It gave his horn a special sound. Duke liked it and encouraged Irvis to keep using it. Later Irvis also used a crushed tomato can as a mute. Like Bubber Miley, Irvis was a growler. When Irvis left the band in 1926, Joe "Tricky Sam" Nanton, another expert with the plunger mute who also made the wah-wah sound, replaced him.

The year 1926 saw another important addition to the band—Harry Carney. He came in as a "temporary" replacement for Toby Hardwick and stayed for the next forty-seven years. Carney played the baritone saxophone, an instrument whose deep tone would add an unusual splash of color to almost all the band's music. He could also hold a single note for three or four minutes, much longer than most players. He did this by inhaling through his nose while blowing air out through his mouth at the same time.

Duke was slowly taking on the band's leadership, at least from the artistic side. He was now writing much of the music for the group. Just as Duke's fate as an artist was becoming more and more linked to the talents and sound of The Washingtonians, their future was becoming tied to his music.

Another composer might have tried to get the people who played his music to change their playing to suit his style. But Ellington realized that the musicians he worked with were special. So he let the new kind of sound that each musician made influence his writing. It was a practice that would always make Duke's music sound different from what many other composers were writing. It also meant that Ellington's music played by someone else never sounded quite the same as when the composer and his men played Duke's own tunes.

With a popular hot and bluesy sound and a growing reputation, the band was on the brink of stardom. But they were missing a manager who could spend all his time on the business side of things. The man they needed showed up in 1926, talking fast and smoking big cigars. His name was Irving Mills, and he was white. Many black entertainers found that they needed white managers if they were to achieve widespread popularity in America.

Duke Ellington

A PICTURE PORTFOLIO

DUKE ELLINGTON'S

Piano Solos

PRICE
$1.00

CONTENTS ★

A dance number featuring Gregg Bruge (left), Mercedes Ellington (center), and Northern Calloway (right), from the 1988 Broadway revival of *Sophisticated Ladies*, a musical tribute to Duke Ellington's work. Mercedes Ellington is Duke Ellington's granddaughter.

(Above)
Mercer Ellington, Duke's son, receives his Grammy Award in
1987. For years, Mercer managed his father's band, but finally
was recognized for his own contributions to the music world.

(At left)
Duke Ellington in 1969, at age 70 the "grand old man" of jazz

Irving Mills heard the group at the Kentucky Club and told Duke that they should be making records. Mills, who published songs, said he could draw on his connections to get them recorded by labels that usually didn't put out records by black musicians. Ellington signed up Mills as his manager. Duke's ties with Mills and the powerful connection it gave him in the music business now made it official: the band had become Duke Ellington's.

The influence that Mills had on the early Ellington band went beyond just looking after the group's business interests. Mills had a good idea of what people wanted to hear. He edited some of Duke's music, simplifying the arrangements. He told Ellington what kinds of songs were most likely to sell. He even added some of his own ideas to the music and lyrics. In return, Mills's name appeared with Ellington's on the sheet music of many of the songs Duke composed. They included some of Ellington's best sellers, such as "Caravan" and "Sophisticated Lady." That meant that Mills got a good share of the income from each piece of sheet music and record sold.

Mills also helped Duke to get down to the business of writing music. Ellington once wrote that "without a deadline, I can't finish nothing." Irving Mills put just enough pressure on him so that he had to write. Later, some people would say that Mills took advantage of Ellington, and that he was making money unfairly from someone else's work. But Duke never said that.

Hiring Mills appeared to have been a good move. No matter how good the band was, not enough people would have heard of Duke Ellington and his band unless someone helped bring them to the public's attention. Mills also had a deep respect for Duke's work. Duke Ellington, he said, was "the first American composer to catch in his music the true jazz spirit."

The Savoy Ballroom in Harlem could accommodate several thousand dancers on its huge dance floor.

Ellington and his band were trying to make it in the midst of some strong competition. Big-band jazz was a new field in the mid-1920s. However, one group was already making its mark, and Ellington was well aware of it. "The height of my ambition," Duke later said of this period, "was naturally to sound like

Fletcher Henderson." Henderson was a year older than Duke and, like him, a piano player. Henderson had also come to New York in the early 1920s. He had played piano with many famous blues singers and then started a dance band. But people really began to know about him in 1924 when he hired trumpeter Louis Armstrong for his group.

By 1926 the Henderson band was at the top in New York. That year his group opened the Savoy Ballroom, a beautiful Harlem dance hall. Several thousand people could pack its 250- by 50-foot dance floor. It had two bandstands at either end of the room. Often two bands would compete during the evening to see who the crowd liked better. Much of the country heard radio broadcasts from the Savoy. The sound of the bands that played there—especially Henderson's—*was* jazz to many people.

Early recordings, such as "If You Can't Hold the Man You Love" and "You've Got Those Wanna Go Back Again Blues," issued in 1926, didn't sell. With the addition of a trumpet and clarinet, the band was somewhat bigger for recording sessions than it was when they were playing live. The kind of music they played sounded very much like that played by Fletcher Henderson's orchestra. But the Henderson group sounded better because it had some of the best musicians and song arrangements of their time. Duke's piano solos on his early recordings resemble those played by many others then playing the blues. But before the end of 1927, Duke Ellington and his orchestra had produced at least three important recordings that struck off in a new direction. These records would give Duke his own sound. From here on, Duke Ellington's sound was like no one else's.

One of these recordings, "Black and Tan Fantasy" featured the growling and "wah-wah" sound of Bubber

Miley, who was listed on the sheet music as the composer, along with Duke. At one point on the record it sounds almost as if Miley were preaching a sermon through his horn. It was also the first of many of Duke's pieces that would celebrate the culture of black people—in this case, by echoing the gospel singing heard in black churches.

Many people hearing "Creole Love Call," another of Duke's new recordings, probably tried to guess what sort of new instrument they were hearing—and got it wrong. What sounded like another growling horn was really the voice of singer Adelaide Hall. She sang with sounds instead of words. Ellington's music was already featuring horns that sounded like voices, so why not have voices sounding like instruments? For most other jazz composers, the use of a voice as an instrument was at least two or three decades away.

The third recording, "East St. Louis Toodle-oo" (pronounced "toad-low"), owed a lot to Bubber Miley, in the writing as well as the playing. Miley liked to come up with musical phrases based on advertising signs he saw. One that caught his eye from a train window was for Lewando, a cleaner. From it, Miley came up with "Oh, lee-wan-do, oh lee-wan-do." Duke, in turn, made the sound and rhythm of this line the basis of "East St. Louis Toodle-oo." The opening and closing of the number were very unusual. The sound was eerie and mysterious, with a saxophone and clarinet playing in the background while Miley growled. It was to be the Duke's theme song for more than ten years.

With these three records, Duke Ellington and his orchestra were blazing a new trail for jazz. It was dance music, and it was easy to listen to, like what Fletcher Henderson was playing. But it also had something different. Henderson's players had great technique. They were experts at reading music. But Duke's music seemed to reach deeper into the spirit of the blues. It touched a level of feeling that most other groups of the time didn't quite reach. Like much of the music Duke was to write from then on, it also caught its listeners by surprise. It didn't follow patterns that people expected. Just when they thought they were going to hear one thing, they heard something else.

These first pieces of Ellington's art were not produced in some quiet, comfortable place. As with most professional jazz musicians, Duke's life was constant work and pressure. There were times when it seemed as if inspiration just wouldn't come. And sometimes it seemed as if the next job and paycheck wouldn't come either. What's more, in the 1920s gangsters owned many of the clubs where musicians worked. It was not unusual for gunfire to be heard at a nightclub. These conditions made it difficult for musicians to lead straight and narrow lives.

One of the biggest problems was drinking. The Ellington band had its share of this. Bubber Miley drank so much that sometimes he would fall asleep under the piano. He left the band in 1929 and died shortly after of tuberculosis.

The band's leader also drank heavily. "I drank more booze than anybody ever," Duke later claimed. He once bragged that he matched two of his musicians drink for drink one night and then carried them both home. He had second thoughts about heavy drinking as he got older and saw what it did to some of his musicians. Eventually, he all but stopped drinking.

The musician's life also made it hard to keep a marriage together. Travel, which the band did a lot of in the 1930s, kept couples apart for long periods. Even when they stayed in one place, the men in the band were often surrounded by beautiful showgirls. The temptations to stray were many. Duke's wife Edna worked for a while at the Kentucky Club, but that didn't save her marriage. Duke fell in love with a showgirl named Mildred Dixon and moved in with her. Edna returned to Washington. Duke and she never divorced, and he continued to support her. But he also never liked to talk about her. In his autobiography, he doesn't even mention her name.

By the end of 1927, Ellington was on the verge of stardom. The band was his, the sound of its music was becoming identified with him, and the public was becoming aware of him. Ellington and the other musicians he worked with had also become a polished show business act.

People who want a career in show business usually need to look like a star as well as have the talent of one. Duke Ellington and his orchestra were beginning to sell many records, but their earnings still depended upon their live shows. What people thought of them when they appeared on the bandstand was important. Ellington looked the part he needed to play. Cab Calloway, another bandleader who became famous at this time, remembered how impressive Duke looked as he neared the age of thirty. "He was a handsome, almost shy-looking man," Calloway recalls, "with his hair brushed straight back and a thin moustache. He wore loose-fitting, comfortable clothes, and he was almost always smiling."

Duke also knew how important it was that his band excite people when they came to see the musicians in person. Although they were fortunate to have steady work at one club during this period, the Ellington orchestra also got the chance to take breaks from their routine and play in local theaters. When they did, Duke made sure they were a feast for the eye as well as the ear.

Cab Calloway, the popular bandleader of the 1930s, was known for his rhythmic scat-singing refrain, "hi-de-hi-de-ho."

At a typical performance, the music would start with a little spectacle. When the curtain went up, the band appeared behind a transparent screen. A blue light shone on them. The musicians looked like ghostly shadows behind the screen, adding atmosphere, color, and mystery to their music. The effect was similar to the lighting at some rock concerts. It added to the crowd's enjoyment.

With his act perfected and his music gaining a reputation for its distinctive sound, Duke was ready for his big break. The Cotton Club, one of Harlem's most important night spots, needed a new band. The position was offered to the Chicago jazz man King Oliver and his band, but he turned it down because it didn't pay enough. The Ellington orchestra was one of five groups that tried out for the job. Duke and his men arrived three hours late for the tryout. But, fortunately for them, so did the man who was doing the hiring. He heard only the Ellington orchestra, liked them, and gave them the job.

The nightclubs in New York featured some of the best black entertainers in the country. But while blacks worked there, they would almost never be admitted as patrons. Although the clubs were in the heart of one of the most important black neighborhoods in America, they had a "whites only" policy. Only black celebrities had a chance of getting in.

Blacks such as Duke Ellington went along with these practices because they had no choice. It was the only way they could become successful. The white gangsters controlled the jobs. And it was important for black artists to reach a white audience if they were to become known outside of their own community.

Ellington hated controversy and didn't want to talk about such things when he didn't have to. In *Music Is My Mistress*, his life story, he ignores the issue of segregation in the clubs. But Cab Calloway, whose band followed Duke's into the Cotton Club, did have something to say about it. Years later he wrote:

> I don't condone it, but it existed and was in keeping with the values of the day. It couldn't happen today. It shouldn't have happened then. It was wrong. But on the other hand, I doubt that jazz would have survived if musicians hadn't gone along with such racial practices there and elsewhere.

The Cotton Club was one flight up, built over a ballroom at the corner of Lenox Avenue and 142nd Street. It was less than two blocks from the Savoy Ballroom. The seating capacity was about 500. The club's stage was set up to look like the outside of a slave cabin on a pre-Civil War cotton plantation. "I suppose the idea was to make whites who came to the club feel like they were being catered to and entertained by black slaves," Calloway wrote.

Ellington preferred to look at the brighter side. According to him, it was "a classy spot." He liked the idea that the club's owners made sure that the customers were well-behaved, no matter how much they drank.

The Cotton Club, however, was not without its unruly patrons. Once a man walked up to Duke and insisted that the band play "Singin' in the Rain."

The King Oliver jazz band featured a young trumpet player, Louis Armstrong, seen here fourth from the left.

The Cotton Club was largely responsible for bringing jazz to a white audience.

Duke hated to be pushed into doing anything. He could be very stubborn when he felt someone was putting pressure on him. At this point one of the owners came over and told Duke that the man was "Legs" Diamond, a famous gangster, and that he had just murdered somebody in an argument. According to Barney Bigard, who then played clarinet in the band, "Next thing you know we were playing 'Singin' in the Rain' for a whole hour. . . ."

Ellington took this gangster business very seriously, and he quickly learned to make his peace with it, especially after threats were made to kidnap him. One gangster, Jerry Sullivan, took a liking to Duke. After the kidnapping threats, he drove Duke to work in his bullet-proof car. During the ride Sullivan kept a sub-machine gun on his lap.

Not long before Duke opened at the Cotton Club, whites had very little to do with black culture. Now it was all the rage. White writers, such as playwright Eugene O'Neill, were giving blacks important roles in their works. For a while, rich white people subsidized black writers, such as Langston Hughes. Whites came uptown to hear the new music for the same reasons that they now wanted to see African art. It seemed exotic—foreign and mysterious.

Before, black culture was seen as inferior. Now many white people thought that black people had a kind of liveliness and spirit lacking in whites. So whites went up to Harlem to experience this excitement.

The shows at the Cotton Club played up the appeal that black culture now had for whites. The showgirls and dancers dressed in what people thought of as African clothing. They tried to create an effect that seemed almost primitive. The music that Ellington was composing and playing, with its growling horns and deep wah-wah sound, was called "jungle music." Some of the tunes he wrote even had the word "jungle" in the title. Among them were "Jungle Nights in Harlem" and "Jungle Blues." Again, Duke was in luck since his style fit right into the spirit of the moment.

Duke's biggest break came when the new CBS radio network ran a wire to the club and began broadcasting from it. The shows were broadcast frequently. This

The Ellington band just before their opening at the Cotton Club in 1927.

brought Ellington to the attention of people all over the country, building him a national reputation.

When Ellington moved his band to the Cotton Club, he expanded it from five to eleven musicians. They played seven nights a week, working from 9 P.M. to 3 A.M., with a short break every hour. They provided the music for two shows each night and played dance music in between.

Ellington added several more musicians to the band in the four years it played at the Cotton Club. Many of his players stayed together for over ten years until the beginning of the 1940s. This made it possible for Duke to write music to suit the talents of band members whose abilities he got to know very well. Together they created what we know today as the Ellington sound.

The most important new members were Johnny Hodges, Barney Bigard, and Cootie Williams. Hodges came from Boston and played the alto saxophone. His beautiful tone could reduce some people to tears. He played straight from his soul. His horn became a vital part of the band. Bigard, from New Orleans, was one of the best clarinet players of his day. He was known for his "woody" tone, which became one of the sounds that Duke could draw on when he composed. Cootie Williams had played trumpet in the Fletcher Henderson band. He was a fine musician, but the other stars in the Henderson group overshadowed him. Williams wanted to play solos and with Duke he got his chance. Duke also wanted something else from Cootie, but he didn't tell him directly. Duke told him, "Just do what feels right to you." It took some time before Williams realized that the growls and "wah-wahs" that Bubber Miley used to make would now be his job.

The musicians whose artistry was now at Duke's command formed more than just a jazz orchestra. In Ellington's hands, they would be a finely tuned instrument. With them, he would create new sounds and strike out in new directions in the composition of jazz. The music he created influences jazz to this day.

The Duke in 1934 had already toured England, where he and his band were treated like royalty.

CHAPTER 3

AN ARTIST EMERGES: *1927-1935*

Duke Ellington always stressed the importance of luck in his career, but all the luck in the world would have meant nothing if he hadn't had something special to offer people when the breaks came along. He did have talent, and he used it to produce a body of work that would place him in the upper ranks of America's composers, jazz and classical.

The way Duke composed differs from classical music composers, who write their music without worrying about which musicians will play it. If the orchestra and conductor are professionals, the music sounds much the same each time. But jazz composers have to deal with the fact that the musicians who will play their pieces are also like composers. They improvise; that is, they make up parts as they go along. So Duke had the job of getting his band to play what he wrote the way he wanted to hear it while letting his musicians also contribute to the creative process.

Classical composers actually write the music down on paper and later the orchestra plays it. Ellington often skipped much of the writing part. He composed *with* his orchestra. The band rehearsal was just as creative a time as when he was composing by himself. You might say his musicians were really co-composers, and their names often appeared next to Duke's on many of his published songs.

The Ellington band truly worked together. "He thought of the band as a unit," Barney Bigard recalls. When Duke asked Barney to join the group, he called it "our" band and always said "we" when talking about it. When he thought about hiring somebody new, he asked his musicians in the band for their opinions.

Duke would sketch out an idea for a song before bringing it to his musicians. He didn't write out all the music. Rather, he might tell Johnny Hodges that he wanted something a little sad and bluesy from his saxophone to go with an opening that Duke played on the piano. Hodges would blow a few notes and then Duke might say, "Yeah, but a little softer; and draw it out a little." He often used painting terms to describe the "color" of his music. He might even say to a musician, "Make it pastel." Then Hodges would say, "How about this?" And then he would play his part again, taking into account what Duke wanted. After more of this going back and forth they would finally get it just right. Sometimes the notes he got from one of the band members would later inspire him to write another song.

Duke later said of this process: "Music can be or-
chestrated without being written. Notes can be given
orally to the musicians. You say to one: 'You play da-
dada-da.' To the next one, 'do-dodo-da.' To another,
'de-dada-da.' Then altogether, 'Ahrrrhmmmmm!'
That's arranging."

Sometimes Duke would have to reach for some kind
of comparison to let a musician know what he wanted
to hear. At one session, he let Cootie Williams know
what he had in mind like this: "Hey Coots, you come
in growling softly like a hungry little lion cub that
wants his dinner but can't find his mother."

With his larger band Duke now had several trumpets, saxophones and, eventually, trombones to create
parts for. He concentrated on getting the part for the
lead instrument in each group to sound the way he
wanted it to. But the second and third members of
each band section would often have to come up with
their own notes. Lawrence Brown, who came in a little
later as the third trombonist, remembered that "you
just went along and whatever you heard was missing,
that's where you were."

Once the musicians in each section had worked out
their part, they got together by themselves to practice.
Then Duke would make further changes when the
whole band came together to play the piece. "A little
more trumpet, talk to me with your trombone," he
might call out as he fine-tuned the music. Then, when
it sounded like it was coming together, he might tell
them: "Give your heart! Let go your soul!" And the
result would be another Duke Ellington classic.

A classical composer like Beethoven never would
have done it this way. He would have written out all
the parts, telling each musician exactly what he was to
do. Giving up so much power to the musicians would
have been out of the question. Even other bandleaders

of Duke's time—like Benny Goodman and Glenn Miller just a few years later—were more likely to insist on doing everything their own way. But then they would be playing music someone else composed. It was rare for the composer and bandleader to be the same person.

Irving Mills would have been happier if Duke had done things a little bit more like Beethoven. Mills complained that it was hard to get the valuable sheet music from Duke's songs since so many of them were worked out with the band and only written down if somebody who was good at reading and writing music sat in on the sessions. Later Duke hired a copyist to do this job full-time. This person translated what the band was playing into written notes.

Billy Strayhorn, an arranger and composer who later worked closely with Duke, once said that "Ellington plays the piano, but his real instrument is his band." And Duke played this "instrument" carefully. When writing for it, he kept in mind each musician's strengths and weaknesses. The trick was not to worry about their weak spots but to blend what they did best. "Any time you have a problem, you have an opportunity," was how Duke looked at it.

Duke always felt that emotions were more important than technique. What a composer needed to remember was not scales but feelings. For Duke those feelings often came from memories. For example, one song came from a memory of when he was "a little boy in bed and heard a man whistling on the street outside, his footsteps echoing away."

In putting those feelings into his music, Ellington was not afraid to be different. For instance, most composers first write their melody and then figure out the harmony—the chords that will be played with the tune. But Duke often created the chords first. This was part of his genius. His greatest contribution to jazz lay in the new and unusual harmonies he developed, but it also kept him from writing more hit tunes than he might have had he worked the way others did. The public liked simple melodies they could whistle or hum. Much of Duke's writing was anything but simple.

Duke liked to experiment with sound, another trait that set him apart from the other bandleaders. He loved to fool around, combining notes that weren't usually played together. He liked it as much when these notes sounded odd—different from what people expected to hear—as when they sounded natural. These sounds seemed to add a nice color to the music. This orchestral color enabled him to paint pictures with sound, suggesting images and feelings through music.

Duke also came up with unusual combinations of instruments to get the sounds and moods he wanted— what Billy Strayhorn called the "Ellington effect." Duke used some instruments in his pieces in ways that people hadn't heard before. For example, in one part of "East St. Louis Toodle-oo," a saxophone plays with a tuba to produce an uncommon sound. He would also use a whole section of his band, such as the trumpets, the way others would use a soloist. Duke was also the first to use the baritone saxophone as a solo instrument.

Duke's musicians were sometimes just as surprised as the audience when they first heard his ideas. Barney Bigard remembers playing parts on his clarinet that he expected to be given to other instruments. At first it seemed strange, but after a while, when he heard the result, it made a lot of sense.

The Ellington effect was crucial to the band's success. Bands like Fletcher Henderson's often got their sound by having the brass and reed instruments pitted against each other. First one section would play part of the music, then the other would repeat it or play a variation on it. This was known as "call and response." The brass, for example, would "call," and the reeds would "respond." Duke did something different. He blended the instruments, whether brass with reeds or a soloist with the orchestra. This blend helped to give his music its "color," and a greater emotional power than other kinds of big band jazz.

Russell Procope, who later played clarinet and also sax in the band, once talked about this special Ellington sound. He said that people "can't put their finger on it, but they *hear* the difference." Duke called it "mixtures." "It's like somebody baking a cake or scrambling eggs," he said. "You mix it up."

It's always hard to say why one artist tries a new path and others don't. In Duke's case, it may have had something to do with his personality. He loved to go against whatever the experts said was right. Jazz critic Stanley Dance, who was close to Ellington, said that Duke "always liked to do something which they said was wrong." He also hated to do the same thing twice in a song, so he had to keep coming up with new twists.

Will Marion Cook, a songwriter, arranger, and musician, had told Duke early in his career: "First you find the logical way, and when you find it, avoid it, and let your inner self break through and guide you. Don't try to be anybody else but yourself." Apparently Duke listened to him.

Gunther Schuller, who composes both jazz and classical music and also writes about jazz, has another idea about how Duke's style reflected his personality. He compares the way Duke blended musical colors to hiding the sounds behind a veil. It made the music

The Ellington band upon its arrival in Southampton, England, 1933.

mysterious, and it wasn't always easy to figure out which particular instruments on a record were making which sounds. This resembled the way Duke acted and spoke in public. He never quite let interviewers pin him down. He made it hard for people to know just what he was thinking. He put up a veil, almost a mask, in front of his private self.

Duke probably also experimented because of the variety of music he had to write while at the Cotton Club. The shows kept changing. Every time they did,

Duke had to write new music for them. He had to keep coming up with new ideas so that each show would be different from the others.

Duke's early study of art may also have influenced the special sound of his music. Mercer Ellington says that his father "never left color when he switched from painting to music." Duke was aware of this. "I like to see the flames licking yellow in the dark and then pushing down to a red glow," he said about his thoughts while composing a song.

Duke had a visual imagination. He thought in terms of pictures as well as sound. Often he was able to convert what he saw into sound. He could also make his music reflect what other people saw. This talent is sometimes found in his comments about other musicians. Duke once wrote about Chick Webb, a famous drum player and bandleader of the early 1930s, "Some musicians are dancers. Chick Webb painted pictures of dances with his drums."

Music lovers in America and abroad took quickly to the Ellington sound. By 1930, Duke's new approach to music was beginning to produce some hits. The big hit of 1930 was "Mood Indigo," which is now a classic. This work is like a classical composer's tone poem—it captures a mood or feeling with music.

The original title of this piece was "Dreamy Blues," but it got linked to Duke's favorite color, blue (of which indigo is a shade). The mood of the song is simple. As Duke put it:

> Just a story about a little girl and a little boy. They are about eight and the girl loves the boy. They never speak of it, of course, but she just likes the way he wears his hat. Every day he comes to her house at a certain time and she sits in her window and waits. Then one day he doesn't come. "Mood Indigo" just tells how she feels.

To give this music its "blue" tone, Duke had a trumpet, clarinet, and trombone carry the melody together. Both the trumpet and trombone were played with mutes. Barney Bigard, who helped Duke write the music, had a featured solo. Freddie Guy's banjo kept the beat. The public loved it, and "Mood Indigo" turned out to be Duke's first real hit.

In 1931 Duke Ellington wrote something that at the time seemed very unusual. Today we wouldn't think twice about a jazz composition that takes six minutes to play. But back then, jazz tunes were supposed to fit on one side of a record. That meant about three minutes of playing time on the 10-inch, 78-RPM (revolutions per minute) records then in use. Anything more got the people at the record companies very nervous. They didn't think their customers would want to hear—not to mention buy—something that long unless it was classical music. But Irving Mills felt that Duke would get lots of publicity as a "serious" composer if he wrote a longer piece.

The work was called *Creole Rhapsody*. It didn't take Duke long to write it. The band was leaving by train for a date in Chicago, and Mills asked Duke to have it ready to play when they arrived. Duke had composed "Mood Indigo" in fifteen minutes. This one took longer, but he still managed to do it overnight.

Duke Ellington was not the first to write long jazz or jazz-influenced pieces. Scott Joplin, the rag composer, had written an opera with jazz-like elements. James P. Johnson had produced symphonies and concertos with a heavy jazz influence. But none of their works were a success. Then, in 1924, the public first heard George Gershwin's *Rhapsody in Blue*. It was classical music with echoes of jazz. It lasted about twenty minutes. A similar piece, *The Grand Canyon Suite*, was written by Ferde Grofé, an arranger for the Paul Whiteman band.

So Duke's *Creole Rhapsody* didn't come out of nowhere. But unlike Gershwin's and Grofé's work, it was pure jazz. And unlike the longer pieces by Joplin and Johnson, Duke's first try got a lot of attention.

Creole Rhapsody was music to listen to—like classical music. It was not dance music because the tempo kept changing. It went back and forth from slow to fast. The piece lasted long enough to give many of the musicians a solo, including the piano player. Duke had two long piano solos on this record.

Aside from being longer than his other music, *Creole Rhapsody* was also important because of what was happening to the solo parts. Duke's music had often been a background against which musicians like Bubber Miley could "show their stuff." The solo parts and the music played behind them were not fully tied together. Now Duke was really calling the tune. His personality was in every part of the music. And his music was starting to seem more and more like a painting in which all the parts blended together to make one, beautiful image.

This blending of the different parts also created a certain tension in the music. Jazz is an art of individuals. Solos and improvisation are at the center of it. The jazz soloist is as much a composer as the person who writes the music. In the Ellington band, it was as if there was a constant tug-of-war between the genius of each player and the genius of their leader, the composer. This was not a bad thing. Great art is often created out of such tension. And Duke Ellington was creating great art with his orchestra.

Duke felt another kind of tension in these and later years. He was an artist who also had to make a lot of money. He had moved his parents, sister, and son into a Harlem apartment and had to support them. The neighborhood in which they lived was called Sugar

Hill. That's because it took a lot of "sugar" (money) to live there.

Keeping his band together also meant large expenses and a big payroll. So while he created jazz masterpieces, Duke also had to make sure that his orchestra was earning its keep. That meant traveling around the country for personal appearances as well as making records. It also meant turning out a lot of popular music that some of his fans and critics thought was a little too superficial.

Although the band had steady work at the Cotton Club into 1931, that wasn't their only showcase. In 1929 they played music written by George Gershwin in the Broadway production of *Show Girl*. The band also made a movie short based on Duke's "Black and Tan Fantasy."

In 1931, the same year he wrote *Creole Rhapsody*, Ellington hired a female singer for his band. It was Irving Mills's idea. He thought it would make the band more popular. But the person Mills first had in mind was not hired because her skin was too light and some people might have thought she was white. At the time, people would not have approved of a white woman singing with a black band. Sonny Greer's wife knew a singer who had worked at the Cotton Club. She was good and she had dark skin, so they hired her.

The singer was Ivie Anderson, who was to stay with the band until 1942. She became an important part of its stage shows. Ivie would come on stage dressed all in white. During her performance she would delight the audience by kidding around with Sonny Greer, who would call out to her from behind his drums. But her singing was moving as well as fun. Her specialty was the song "Stormy Weather." When Ivie sang that song, Duke said, people would be "crying and applauding."

Ivie Anderson was the lead singer with the Ellington band from 1931 until 1942.

The band's fame was increasing. With hits like "Rockin' in Rhythm," "Sophisticated Lady," and "It Don't Mean a Thing If It Ain't Got That Swing," America was dancing to Duke's tunes. The Ellington band was hot, which sometimes meant that its leader had to put up with a good deal of heat.

With fans and critics closely watching everything he did, Duke had to make at least some people unhappy once in awhile. That happened when he hired Lawrence Brown as the group's third trombone player to join Tricky Sam Nanton and Juan Tizol. It was the first time a jazz orchestra had so many players on that instrument. Some critics saw Brown's hiring as a big mistake. They thought they knew what kinds of players fit in best with Duke's style. Brown, they said, had too sweet a tone; he wasn't "bluesy" enough.

Duke hired Brown on Irving Mills's advice. "I never met you, never heard you," Ellington told Brown. "But Irving says get you, so that's that." Brown acted as well as sounded different from some of the other players. He didn't smoke, drink, or gamble. He was also a little cranky and hard to get along with. But his playing on the band's recordings for years afterward shows that Mills was right. Brown's sweet tones added still another color to Duke's music.

Duke also had to put up with some complaints from the critics in 1933. This time their criticism had to do with the music that Duke played on his first trip abroad. Irving Mills, always looking to spread Ellington's fame, booked Duke into the London Palladium. At the time it was one of the most famous showplaces in the world.

Upon arriving in England, Ellington and his men met a familiar problem. A London newspaper checked to see if they would be able to get hotel rooms. Its reporter called several hotels and asked if they accepted black guests. "We can put one up for the night if he's well-behaved," the manager of one place said. "Is he very black?" asked a clerk at another. Duke, who was light-skinned, managed to get a room. But the rest of the band had to stay in small places outside of London.

In other ways, however, the band was treated royally. In fact, they were treated that way by royalty. The Prince of Wales, later to become the King of England, was one of their fans. He attended a private party at which the band played. His Highness admired Sonny Greer's drums and by the end of the evening he and Greer were friends. The prince called

him "Sonny" and Greer called the prince "The Whale."
The Whale even took a turn at Sonny's drums. "Good
hot drums," Duke said about his playing. Later when
the prince went to one of the band's theater concerts,
instead of sitting in the special royal box, he decided to
sit where everyone else was—down in the audience
with the rest of Duke's fans.

At their concerts in Great Britain, the band looked
striking. They wore cream-colored suits with orange
ties and brown shoes. On the whole, the British audiences loved Duke's music, but there were still many
people who were not familiar with it. At one of the
concerts people laughed at the growling sound made
by Cootie Williams's trumpet and Tricky Sam Nanton's trombone. In response, Duke had the band play
more popular music after the intermission. It featured
sweeter sounds—sounds that were easier to listen to.

Some British reviewers criticized Ellington for playing down to the audience. They had come to hear the
great and original jazz artist, the Duke Ellington who
had been invited to lecture at New York University
and play at Columbia University, the genius who had
already been invited to the White House along with
other important people in black culture. These critics
thought that for Duke to play popular music just to
satisfy the crowd was a step down for him.

Duke had other ideas. He knew that he was an
entertainer as well as an artist. People had paid to
hear him and his musicians. And he was going to
bring his music to these people in whatever way they
could enjoy it.

He would also bring it to wherever they lived. Jazz
musicians were becoming very popular throughout
the United States, and Ellington's popularity was
among the highest. Movie theaters were adding stage
shows to their screen presentations. Their owners

were willing to pay a great deal of money for an appearance by Duke and his men, more than the band could make by staying at the Cotton Club. Large nightclubs across America were also beckoning. It was time to move on.

After leaving the Cotton Club in 1931, Ellington and the band spent much of the year traveling. Those were the days before people traveled by plane. The train was still the standard way of going long distances. Irving Mills saw to it that the musicians were as comfortable as possible when they traveled. When they were going to be on the road for a long period of time, he rented special railroad cars for them. Depending on the size of the band, they would have either one or two cars for the players and one for their baggage and instruments.

The band members had upper and lower sleeping berths in their car. They passed the time on the train by playing cards—and by playing tricks on each other. One favorite prank was putting itching powder in another musician's clothing.

Duke always had a separate compartment to himself. In later years, he would spend less and less private time with his musicians. But in the early 1930s he still drank and played cards with them on the long trips between cities. It helped to keep the band close and loyal to each other.

Night was Duke's composing time, his working hours. As the train rushed down the track through the darkness, he spent many hours coming up with ideas for new pieces. He jotted them down on whatever was handy, even on a paper bag. Almost anything around him could inspire a composition. The song "Daybreak Express" is a good example of this. Barney Bigard remembers the train's whistle tooting at crossings. "Duke would hear all the same things," he recalls.

"The only difference was, we were playing poker, and he was writing music about the whistling."

The band had traveled to a lot of places, but they had avoided the South. When his band first became famous, Duke Ellington was offered a lot of money to take it on a tour of the South. "I don't care," he said. "I won't go south." He didn't want his musicians to have to put up with the segregation of black people in the South at the time—separate hotels, bathrooms, water fountains, lunch counters, and a general lack of respect toward anyone with black skin. He probably had in mind the sort of treatment given Earl Hines, one of the great jazz pianists. When Hines took his band to Fort Lauderdale, Florida, the police made them walk in the gutter instead of on the sidewalk.

But by 1934 Duke had changed his mind. Touring England made him more confident that the band could get along without too much trouble, even when away from the more comfortable northern cities in the United States. He also knew that his musicians could usually avoid the problem of finding a decent hotel that would take them by sleeping on the train.

Despite these precautions, the shadow of racial prejudice dogged the band's tour. In Texas and Missouri, Ellington fans came by the thousands to hear his music, but once off stage, the musicians were poorly treated. "In Europe we were treated like royalty," said Harry Carney. "In Texas, we were back in the colored section." In one town there was a special curfew for blacks. They had to be off the streets by 10 P.M. But the dance at which the band was playing was over later than that. Some of the musicians walking back to the train from the ballroom were stopped by the police.

The rough life on the road made the brief stays at home attractive. Duke seldom had time to relax in his own apartment in these years. But when he did, it was on Harlem's Edgecombe Avenue, where he had moved his family into a five-room apartment. Having his mother there made his life easier.

When Duke and Edna were first married and living in Washington, his mother used to help smooth over the couple's arguments. But in the early days in New York, her calming influence wasn't there, which may have speeded up Duke and Edna's split. By 1934, Duke was separated from Edna and living with dancer Mildred Dixon. Daisy Ellington had moved to New York by this time helping to keep Mildred and Duke's relationship peaceful. Although Mildred and Duke never actually married, Daisy treated her like a daughter-in-law.

Duke needed peace and quiet. He didn't want to get involved in any conflicts—not with anyone. His family knew it and shielded him from the frictions of life as much as they could. He, in turn, gave them a good life. His parents had barely been middle class in Washington, D.C. Now that their son was successful, they lived in upper-class style. Duke not only bought them a Pierce-Arrow, one of the better cars of the day, but also hired a driver. Ruth Ellington, Duke's teenage sister, was probably the best-dressed girl in her school.

As long as Duke had money, he was willing to spend it on those close to him. Music is what he gave his thoughts and energy to—money was to make and to spend. He lived well throughout his life, but he never had much money in the bank.

Unfortunately, his relationship with women, like his relationship with money, was not something Duke Ellington took care of. Duke took after his father in his dress and manners, and he copied the older man's ways with women. Although his father treated his wife well, he always had an eye for other women. If

Duke's sister Ruth Ellington at age sixteen.

anything, Duke may have had an even greater attraction to beautiful women. He did not hesitate to romance them. Handsome, like his father, Duke also had his talent for saying just the right thing to a woman about the way she looked. He was never able to be true to one woman, and he was never able to give the woman he lived with a satisfying relationship.

His trouble with women often spilled over to his relationship with his musicians. Some of his lovers were girlfriends of the members of the band. The musicians, of course, resented this, and at least two of them, Barney Bigard and Juan Tizol, threatened to physically attack him if he didn't stop it.

The constant traveling and the demands of his music didn't help Duke to be the perfect father, either. Although raised by Duke's mother in Washington, D.C., his son Mercer began to take some trips with the band when he was eight. Mercer called the musicians "uncle" and soon was able to work for them, carrying their baggage. But he would have liked more attention from his dad. He couldn't understand why he didn't get it even when Duke was in New York, where Mercer was now living. He wondered why Duke couldn't be with him more often, "why he [his father] would have to stay up late, bang on the piano, and sleep all day."

For Duke Ellington, fame had its price. Almost all his energies went into the creation of his music. That didn't leave much for other people—except in brief bursts. So it made sense that when he later wrote the story of his life, he called it *Music Is My Mistress*.

Duke and his band in 1937. They brought elegance and style to jazz.

CHAPTER 4

THE SWING
YEARS:
1935-1945

Duke's mother died of cancer in 1935. This loss shattered him. "I have no ambition left," he said after she died. "The bottom's out of everything."

Not quite everything, though. Not his music. It was there that he could always express himself. So he poured out his sorrow in a new composition called *Reminiscing in Tempo*. The recording featured Cootie Williams's trumpet. It was Duke's first long piece since *Creole Rhapsody*, taking up four record sides. In it Duke was trying to deal with his mother's death. "It begins with pleasant thoughts," he said of *Reminiscing in Tempo*. "Then something gets you down. Then you snap out of it. . . ." The upbeat ending meant that life had to go on, even after a terrible loss.

Many jazz critics disliked the piece. One called it too "arty." Others complained that there was no improvisation and that it was not real jazz. Duke was hurt by the attacks on his music, although he wouldn't admit it openly. In response, he didn't write another long piece until 1943.

The upheavals in Duke's personal life were mirrored by changes in society. By the early 1930s the country was going through hard times. The Great Depression had hit, and many people had lost their jobs. When they listened to music, they wanted to hear something soft and soothing.

Americans seemed ready for something new in their music. They got it, but it was really something old wrapped up in a new package. The new sound was called "swing." Nobody ever seemed to know exactly what swing was. But they knew it when they heard it.

At first, the bands that the public acclaimed as great swing groups were white. This made things a little rough, at least for a while, for many of the black jazz musicians who had become famous in the 1920s. But the Ellington band kept doing well. Besides making money from concerts, sheet music, and records, they also appeared in several more movies.

The public may not have realized that the white swing bands were building on what black musicians had been doing since the 1920s. Swing was the sound of a big band playing jazz or jazz-like tunes with a steady, driving rhythm. In effect, the Fletcher Henderson band of the 1920s was an early version of a swing group. In swing, the arrangement of the music was important—Henderson's specialty. The trumpets and trombones, especially, had to play together with a flashy sound. Each instrument had to sound like it was adding to the beat that drove the tune on, that made the music "swing." That driving beat made listeners want to clap their hands and dance. It was exciting, and in that way it was like good rock-and-roll music.

By the early 1930s, other black bands playing this type of music had begun to appear. Drummer Chick Webb led one of them. Because rhythm was what made swing swing, drummers were becoming more and more important, and Webb was one of the best. Despite a physical disability—he had a hunchback—he became one of America's favorite musicians.

An increasing number of white musicians were now playing big band jazz. Several of them gained experience in white bands of the late 1920s and early 1930s, such as the Jean Goldkette Orchestra, the Casa Loma Orchestra, and the Paul Whiteman Orchestra. Among these musicians were people like Tommy Dorsey, Glenn Miller, and Benny Goodman. If this kind of music was to catch on, giving musicians who played it a chance to make good money, whites in huge numbers would have to grow to like it. They, after all, had the money to spend on records. When a white band playing this kind of music suddenly became very popular, "swing" became the word on everyone's lips. This music that had come from the lives of black people suddenly spread like a prairie fire.

In the mid-1950s, rock and roll, based on black rhythm and blues, broke through to whites when Elvis Presley made it popular. Clarinetist Benny Goodman is the man who did the same for swing. Part of his success came from playing arrangements by Fletcher Henderson. Henderson didn't actually play with Goodman, but by writing out the musical parts for each instrument, he gave the Goodman band some of the sound that his own group had had in the 1920s.

In 1935 the Goodman band, as part of a national tour, played at the Palomar Ballroom in Los Angeles. The crowd there got so excited by their music that the newspapers picked it up. Before long, everybody was talking about this music. Benny Goodman soon became known as "The King of Swing."

The swing craze took everyone by surprise, including Duke Ellington, even though Duke was one of the first to use the word "swing" in the song title "It Don't Mean a Thing If It Ain't Got That Swing." George Avakian, a jazz critic, said that Duke's music was a kind of "lazy swing." Duke's tempo was slower than that of the fast, hard driving swing bands.

Although he played an important part in creating the music that became swing, Ellington could never be categorized. No label could ever fully describe the music he wrote because it was richer and more complicated than what others were playing. Most swing bands just tried to play hit tunes. And since their leaders weren't composers, they played other people's music. Duke, on the other hand, tried to create his own music whenever he could.

Although Duke continued to be a success, the newer bands got most of the public's attention over the next few years. The swing bands, after all, were new. Ellington had been around for a while. These bands even scored hits with some of Duke's own music, outselling his own band's versions of his songs "Solitude" and "In a Sentimental Mood."

Duke didn't talk much about this, but losing the spotlight to other bands clearly bothered him. He said there was much more to his music than what a person could hear from the newer bands. "Swing is stagnant and without a future," Duke claimed when it first became popular. It was "like the monotonous rhythmical bouncing of a ball. After you hear so much, you get sick of it because it hasn't enough harmony and there isn't enough to it." He played "Negro folk music," he insisted, which had "color, harmony, melody and rhythm," and it would last longer than the currently popular swing. He was right.

Benny Goodman at the Waldorf-Astoria ballroom, 1938.

Irving Mills's job, however, was to make sure that people were still thinking of Duke. So Mills began to promote the band as a swing group. He encouraged Duke to give interviews to reporters to keep music fans reading about him and his band.

Through it all, Duke kept right on composing. Changes in the band meant that Duke would have new sounds to work with while losing others. Musicians left for several reasons—offers of more money from other bands, the chance to play more solos with other groups, or the desire to get married and settle down in one place.

Trumpet player Arthur Whetsol had returned to the band, but in 1934 he became very ill and had to leave again. Duke replaced him with Rex Stewart. Stewart was still another musician whose individual talent added to the Ellington sound. Stewart's specialty was the nasal tone he got from his cornet by pushing down its valves only halfway when he played a note.

In 1936, with the band's Puerto Rican trombonist, Juan Tizol, Duke wrote "Caravan," which had a Latin American sound. Jazz groups still play it today. Ellington also began to write a series of what he called "concertos." These pieces were not exactly like what the classical composers wrote. They were short—short enough to fit on one side of a record. But like the classical concerto, they featured the playing of a soloist against the background of the orchestra.

Meanwhile, swing was causing a stir. Many older people didn't like it. They said that it made young people act wild. One conductor of classical music said that swing led to juvenile delinquency. In an interview Duke, now more at peace with the new music, was asked about the effect of swing on young people. He said that while music *can* get people a little excited, "so do checkers and ping-pong."

Another death in his family again set Duke back. In 1937, his father died. He was only fifty-eight. J.E. had developed a bad cough, which turned out to be tuberculosis. Again Duke felt despair. This time he stopped writing music for a while, although he still led his band. It seemed that one loss after another was disrupting his life. His friend Arthur Whetsol was also dying. Another musician in the band, Freddie Jenkins, was gravely ill, and it looked like he would soon die.

Another dramatic change occurred in Duke's life about this time. After several years, he and Mildred Dixon split up. Duke had fallen in love with another dancer, Bea "Evie" Ellis. Duke's relationship with Bea would last for the rest of his life. Although he did not stop seeing other women, he seemed more committed to this relationship.

Bea and Duke took a separate apartment, leaving Mercer and his sister Ruth to share the old one. Bea eventually became a mother figure in Duke's family. It took Ruth some time to warm up to the new relationship, but Mercer and Bea immediately took to each other. Mercer, who still saw his real mother regularly, after a time began calling Bea "Ma."

With the death of his parents, Duke became the official head of the Ellington family. He had always been protective of his sister, but now he was even more so. While she liked to be taken care of, Ruth also sometimes felt that he wanted to control her life totally. She commented once, "Edward wouldn't permit me to go anywhere at anytime." Duke wanted her to stay close to home and, as she put it, "be there, like a doll."

Her brother's overprotectiveness some say even led to the breakup of her marriage a few years later. Ruth had married a white writer named Dan James. Duke took him into the family and set the couple up in the music-publishing business despite the fact that Ruth was studying science in college and James wanted to make a living through his writing. When James finally started to earn some money from writing, he wanted to live only on what he made, but Ruth wouldn't leave the music-publishing company, and she and Dan eventually divorced.

In Duke's eyes, it was not money that tied Ruth to the business. According to him, "she is more interested in such honors I may receive than in any large sums of money . . . she is more concerned with its prestige than its profitability." He assumed that at the center of Ruth's life was dedication to him.

During this time Duke Ellington made a new friend who was to be almost like a parent to him. Arthur Logan started out as his doctor but ended up being his closest friend. Anyone who served as Duke's personal doctor would be important in his life. He had especially strong feelings about staying healthy. He also had an odd belief about how to stay well. He thought fresh air was unhealthy. And he gulped down vitamins the way some people chew candy. When he was traveling, he would often call his doctor every morning. Dr. Logan was willing to put up with all of Duke's idiosyncracies.

Another change in Duke's life was the ending of his long relationship with Irving Mills. In 1939, Duke signed with the William Morris Agency, and they took over the management of his career. Duke may have felt some pressure from the outside to leave Mills. There was still a lot of talk about how the white man, Mills, had too much power over Ellington's career and made too much money from Duke's songs and public appearances. Congressman Adam Clayton Powell, Jr., a major spokesman for the cause of civil rights for black people at the time, accused Ellington of being "just a musical sharecropper." He meant that Duke did all the work while someone else was getting most of the profits. Whether this is true is debatable. What is true is that Duke had outgrown Mills. Ellington had learned about the music business, and now he felt that he needed a bigger organization to work for him. Leaving Mills, Duke felt, was his "declaration of independence."

Duke Ellington's position in the jazz world required that he have the very best business management. By the late 1930s, he had established his band as one of the top groups in jazz. He had a large following, even when he didn't have a hit tune that everyone was humming. His fans knew not only the music but also the work of each of the major soloists in the Ellington band. Now small groups from the band—say, five or six musicians—could make their own recordings. They knew they would have an audience. Stars such as Barney Bigard, Cootie Williams, and Johnny Hodges led the groups. Sometimes Duke joined them as the pianist.

Meanwhile, the full orchestra was turning out more classic jazz recordings. These included "Diminuendo and Crescendo in Blue," "Prelude to a Kiss," "Boy Meets Horn," and "I Let a Song Go Out of My Heart." In 1937 and 1938, the Ellington band produced a total of twenty-seven records. One of them featured the band playing "Something to Live For," a tune written by Duke and a man named Billy Strayhorn.

Billy, at five feet three inches, was short in stature but long on talent. He came from Pittsburgh, where at the age of nineteen he heard the Duke Ellington band at the Stanley Theater when it came through on tour. Billy had studied classical music, but soon turned to writing the kind of music that Duke played. He managed to get backstage and play some of his music for Duke, who liked what he heard. Duke told Billy to see him in New York, and the next year Strayhorn took him up on it. It was the beginning of one of the greatest teams in the history of American music.

Billy began to travel with the Ellington band. The musicians loved his sweet and gentle nature, so much so that they nicknamed him "Sweet Pea," after the baby in the "Popeye" comic strip. When the band was at home in New York, Billy lived with Ruth and

Mercer Ellington in their Harlem apartment. He was like a member of the Ellington family.

Strayhorn's work for the Ellington band included his own compositions, such as "Lush Life," arrangements of Duke's compositions, and the many tunes that he and Duke wrote together. They worked so well together that one could easily finish a piece that the other had started. Duke later wrote in his autobiography:

> In music, as you develop a theme or musical idea, there are many points at which direction must be decided, and any time I was in the throes of debate with myself, harmonically or melodically, I would turn to Billy Strayhorn. We would talk, and then the whole world would come into focus.

It was not unusual for somebody to come upon them and hear them talking to each other in their strange language. "Dah de dah," one might say. "Dum dah du dah," the other might reply. And nobody could tell which piece was written by whom without the composer's name on it. Even then, you couldn't be sure about it. Playing the piano was the same. On some of the small group recordings, Billy, not Duke, played the piano. It was hard, if not impossible, to tell them apart.

Duke came to trust Billy's opinions completely. "He was my listener," Duke wrote of him, "my most dependable appraiser. . . ." Many people called Strayhorn Duke Ellington's "alter ego," almost a second version of himself. But Duke put it more vividly. He called Billy "my right arm, my left arm, all the eyes in back of my head, my brainwaves in his head, and his in mine."

Billy Strayhorn knew the work of such classical composers as Ravel and Debussy. Through him these classical composers and their emphasis on orchestral color—the use of sounds to suggest images—may have influenced Ellington. Billy also became Duke's musical chief-of-staff. He helped to rehearse the band

Glenn Miller with his band during a broadcast from a hotel.

and often supervised the group's recording sessions. Duke knew that Billy had the right attitude about the connection between creativity and the final artistic product. "Actually, inspiration comes from the simplest kind of thing, like watching a bird fly," Billy once said. "That's only the beginning. Then the work begins. Oh, goodness! Then you have to sit down and work, and it's *hard*."

One of Billy Strayhorn's compositions, "Take the 'A' Train," written in 1941, became the new theme song of the Ellington band. The tune was named after the New York City subway train that Strayhorn rode from midtown Manhattan to Harlem. He composed part of the piece while on the 'A' train. Some of the city's subway routes were being changed, and the lyrics were actually directions for people who wanted to get to Harlem.

Billy came aboard just before Duke Ellington hit his peak. The band and its leader took off in 1939, and the next several years were to be highly successful. Duke seemed to turn out one masterpiece after another during this period. Why did it happen now? Besides Billy's influence, there is little doubt that the addition of bassist Jimmy Blanton and tenor saxophone player Ben Webster to the band definitely played a role.

Jimmy Blanton has become a legend. In the three years he played with Ellington he "revolutionized bass playing, and it has not been the same since," according to Duke. Before him, the bass player marked time, providing a rhythm background for the other musicians. His role seemed so much less important than the other players' that his instrument was called the "doghouse." That was because the person who played it was far from the center of things.

Blanton managed to coax a melody from his oversized fiddle. This was a new way to use this instrument. From that time on, bass players began to take solos. He also played a more complicated rhythmic background to the music. By changing the fingering of the strings of the bass, he was able to make the notes he played last longer. It made the Ellington band vibrate with an earthy sound. Duke thought enough of Blanton's playing to record a series of duets with him on tunes such as "Sophisticated Lady."

If the band was, as Billy Strayhorn had put it, Duke's instrument, then Jimmy Blanton made it a better one. But Duke should be given credit for knowing a good thing when he heard it and for making good use of it. Rhythm was important to Ellington. As a piano player, he felt his job was to "feed the band with rhythm." Now he had an ally. When he composed, he took this into account.

Blanton was at the beginning of what should have been a great and long career. But it was not to be. Three years after he joined the band, he died of tuberculosis. Like too many great jazz musicians, he died young. He was only twenty-one.

Ben Webster, the other addition to the band, brought the group in line with an important trend in jazz. When jazz first arrived on the scene, the trumpet was its star. Gradually the tenor saxophone also became a major solo instrument. So many great musicians had played this instrument in the 1930s that it was growing in popularity. They played in small groups and with the great swing bands. Two of the best were Coleman Hawkins and Lester Young. Now Duke had Ben Webster, also one of the best.

Webster was the band's first tenor sax player who could be featured in solos. Duke took full advantage of this new color in his musical palette. Webster could swing, and he could also produce a beautiful tone on slow ballads. His instrument was featured on such popular Ellington recordings as "What Am I Here For?" "Just a-Settin' and a-Rockin'," and "Conga Brava." His saxophone is the force that propels "Cotton Tail," an upbeat 1940 tune that made many ballrooms and theaters jump. This piece begins without an introduction and had harmonies like those that would later be heard in the modern jazz style called "bebop."

Sometimes great artists can be difficult to get along with. There were times when Duke had to sidestep Webster's tough side. Ben liked to argue. That, of course, was the very thing Duke was always trying to avoid. One time, for instance, Webster came over to the band's leader in a bad mood. He wanted more money. Duke said to Webster, "But Ben—I can't afford to pay you what you're worth. *Nobody* can."

With Duke's new surge of creativity and Blanton and Webster's talent, many jazz lovers feel that the Ellington band of 1939–1942 was possibly the greatest jazz orchestra ever. It certainly was *one* of the greatest. The core of the band had been together for a decade. Its leader had fully developed his special style, and the group had an audience that waited excitedly for each new record. Everything had come together for Duke Ellington.

In one of his compositions of the early 1940s, Duke paid tribute to the rich life of his own New York City neighborhood. The tune was called "Harlem Air-shaft." The airshaft was the closest that people who lived in tenement buildings got to an inner courtyard. It was a narrow space onto which their windows opened. Duke felt that you could know Harlem through one of its airshafts: "You hear fights, you smell dinner, you hear people making love. You hear intimate gossip floating down. You hear the radio. An airshaft is one great big loudspeaker. You see your neighbor's laundry. You hear the janitor's dogs. . . . You smell coffee. . . . You hear people praying, fighting, snoring."

"Ko-Ko" which Duke also wrote in the early 1940s, like "Cotton Tail," looked ahead to modern jazz, the new music of the late 1940s. Vision—to be able to look ahead of the times—is the mark of a great artist. Miles Davis, one of the great figures of modern jazz, who is still playing his trumpet today, once said: "I think all the musicians should get together one certain day and get down on their knees and thank Duke."

Now in great demand, the band took its show on the road much of the time. After another engagement at the new downtown Cotton Club, they traveled again to Europe. This time they visited several countries— France, Belgium, the Netherlands, Denmark, Norway, and Sweden. On their way to Denmark, Duke and the band had to pass through Germany. They didn't play in that country. It was 1939, and racism was the official policy of the Nazi government.

Back in the United States, it was another round of theaters, ballrooms, and nightclubs. Much of the time they supplied live dance music. When the band played at a dance they often began with a slow number. Then they picked up steam as the evening wore on. One Ellington fan remembers hearing them live in Toronto during these years. He recalls them sounding even better than on their records. The record "captured nothing of the mood, nothing of the feeling, nothing of the surge, the drive, the lift" of their live playing. When they started to play "it was an unexpected explosion of sound; startling, thrilling."

The Ellington band was also exciting to see. Different-colored lights shone on each instrument. And Duke often made a dramatic appearance after the concert was underway. He knew how to build suspense. His entry onstage was the signal for the band to move into high gear. They didn't have a set program, except for the first few numbers they played before Duke came out. Once at the piano, from where he led them, Duke called out each number to the band. That way he could see from the mood and reaction of the crowd what they might want to hear.

Almost constantly on the road, Duke and his men lived in an almost closed world—traveling by train or bus to reach engagements, hanging out backstage between performances, grabbing meals when they could, and playing for large and appreciative audiences. But sometimes the outside world intruded.

The early 1940s were important years for all Americans. With the rise of the Nazis in Germany, Americans were becoming more aware of their freedom. It was by no means guaranteed. Suddenly the world didn't seem so safe. Black Americans were just as patriotic as everyone else—many fought and died for their country in World War II. But for many black Americans freedom was not something they could take for granted. Blacks still had to use separate hotels and bathrooms in many states. They were even segre-

From left to right: Dinah Shore, Spike Jones, Count Basie, Bob Burns, Lionel Hampton, and Tommy Dorsey perform on a broadcast to the troops, 1942.

gated—kept in separate units—in the army. And they were prevented from voting in many areas of the country. Many blacks were beginning to ask why.

Lena Horne, a talented and beautiful black singer and a friend of Duke's, found herself doing just that. When she was performing for soldiers at an army base in Arkansas, she noticed that German prisoners of war were in the audience, but black soldiers at the base were kept away. When she saw this, she did the only thing she felt she could do: she walked out.

Ellington and his band often ran into racial barriers during the war years when they were playing at the Fox Theater in St. Louis. They had trouble getting cabs to take them from the train station to the theater. Then, between shows, they couldn't find a nearby place to grab a quick bite to eat. Finally they had to send a white person to a lunch counter to buy some sandwiches for them. All because of the color of their skin.

It wasn't Duke's style to take the kind of direct action that Lena Horne did. Duke felt that things were loosening up between the races, at least in the music world. For instance, it was now becoming okay for blacks and whites to play jazz together. Strange as it may seem, this didn't happen to any great extent until Benny Goodman and his drummer, Gene Krupa, teamed up with black musicians Teddy Wilson and Lionel Hampton to form a quartet in the late 1930s.

Duke's feeling about racial problems were expressed through his music. In 1941 he composed music for a show in Los Angeles that focused on the talents and triumphs of black people: *Jump for Joy*. Duke had been bothered for some time by shows that didn't accurately portray blacks. *Porgy and Bess*, by George and Ira Gershwin, for example, had great music, but it wasn't true to life. The characters in it were not like people you would ever meet on the street. While he liked the music, Duke didn't think that it came out of the experience of blacks in America.

In *Jump for Joy*, Duke took his turn at a musical picture of the spirit of black Americans. The cast, besides the Ellington band and Ivie Anderson, included blues singer Joe Turner, Dorothy Dandridge, who later acted in movies, and Herb Jeffries, whose voice and good looks soon brought him stardom. *Jump for Joy* only ran for twelve weeks. Its importance, however, was not in how many performances it gave but in its portrayal of blacks as real people, not childlike or clownish. It celebrated the death of Uncle Tom, an old stereotype of blacks and the demise of "Jim Crow," the symbol of segregation. The idea, as Duke later wrote, was to "make the audience think."

Jump for Joy's short run might have been because it was ahead of its time. Despite the threat of Nazism and the greater attention now paid to the lack of freedom abroad, white Americans were not ready to accept that millions of people in their own country were not free.

While grappling with the connection between his art and society, Duke was also trying to come to terms with a more personal, artistic problem. Can an entertainer also be an artist? Many people didn't think so. Duke had other ideas, and he was soon to prove his point.

Now one of America's most famous entertainers would have a chance to display his art in a place where the greats of classical music usually performed—Carnegie Hall. Benny Goodman had played there in the late 1930s, but he played the same swing music that was on his records. Duke, on the other hand, took advantage of this opportunity to explore the possibilities of composing and playing a kind of symphonic jazz more complicated than anything else he had done before.

The main work Duke's band played at the Carnegie Hall concert was his *Black, Brown and Beige*, a forty-five-minute piece. In it Duke would do nothing less than give a musical portrait of the experience of blacks in America. He had begun to think of composing an extended work on this subject in the early 1930s. He said then of his intentions: "I am expressing in sound the old days in the jungle, the cruel journey across the sea, and the despair of the landing. And then the days of slavery. I trace the growth of a new spiritual quality and then the days in Harlem. . . ."

The Ellington orchestra gave the concert in January 1943. The critics' reactions were mixed, at best. Some of the jazz magazines liked it. One critic, Leonard Feather, called it "the elevation of jazz to an orchestral art." But most newspaper reviewers were unhappy. They thought Duke was trying to reach too far. The three-minute masterpieces he had been turning out, they felt, did not hold up when woven together into a longer piece. "Mr. Ellington had set himself a lofty goal," wrote one, "and with the best of intentions he did not achieve it."

While this criticism must have hurt Ellington, he obviously gave it some serious thought. Almost a year later he was back at Carnegie Hall with a shortened version of *Black, Brown and Beige*. This is music that jazz fans still listen to today. It is a little more than fifteen minutes long and made up of sections called "Work Song," "Come Sunday," "The Blues," "Three Dances," "Emancipation Celebration," and "Sugar Hill Penthouse."

Despite some occasional negative criticism, the Ellington orchestra was one of the most popular in America. It seemed as if the group's fame would continue to grow, and the well-paying engagements and hit records would go on indefinitely. But this was not to be. Hard times lay ahead.

The Duke with his son Mercer, who eventually took over management of the band.

CHAPTER 5

"THINGS AIN'T WHAT THEY USED TO BE": *1945-1956*

Clearly a big change was in the making even during Ellington's greatest years. Some of the musicians who had helped make the group what it was were leaving. By the mid-1940s, it was hard to recognize the band. Jimmy Blanton had died, and Ivie Anderson had left to settle down and start a business.

Another great loss was Cootie Williams, who left to join Benny Goodman. It was the talk of the jazz world. Duke's star trumpet player had jumped ship, or so it seemed. People thought it so important that band-leader Raymond Scott even wrote a tune called "When Cootie Left the Duke." The story behind it, though, was nothing mysterious. Duke understood that Cootie could make more money and have a good shot at advancing his career by making this move. So Duke didn't make a fuss and wished him well. As it happened, Cootie eventually ended up leading his own band. Years later, he returned to play with Ellington.

Barney Bigard, whose clarinet was an important part of the Ellington sound, got married and decided he had had enough traveling for a while. Toby Hardwick took offense when Duke criticized his girlfriend one day, and simply walked out. Rex Stewart quarreled with Duke and left, and Juan Tizol quit to join the Harry James band at a higher salary than Duke was paying him. Tricky Sam Nanton died.

Ben Webster wasn't getting any easier to get along with and finally left after upstaging the Duke during a performance.

The loss of all these people in just a few years had a profound effect on the Ellington band, even though their replacements were some of the best in the business. Ray Nance on trumpet and Jimmy Hamilton on clarinet, for example, were fine musicians. The same was true for Russell Procope, who also joined the clarinet section. Paul Gonsalves, who came to the orchestra in 1950, would be the featured tenor sax soloist on scores of Ellington records. They would all play with Duke for many years. In Cat Anderson, who came aboard in 1944, the band gained not only a good trumpet player but also a flashy one. Anderson could play high notes that other trumpeters only dreamed of. When he did, he would point upward, as if he were showing the audience where the note he was reaching for was located.

The sound coloration of each musician is unique and, like a painter, Duke counted on knowing what colors were in his palette. An orchestra that was beginning to seem different almost daily made it harder for Duke to compose. It had taken him a long time to get to know his players well enough so that he could create the final versions of his work with them in rehearsals. When musicians left, his connection to the band—his instrument—was disrupted.

In a 1962 interview, Duke reflected on this problem: "A certain sound comes out of a big band. It may be the character given it by a large brass section, or by a particularly skillful group of saxophones. The minute you change the men in the section, it doesn't sound the same, although you may have the same arranger."

In fact, the band would never again be as stable as it was throughout the 1930s. In the trumpet section alone, fifteen different musicians would play in the period from 1942 to 1949. Later it got worse. Twenty-two trumpeters sat in those chairs from 1960 to 1974.

Turnover in the band would be a constant problem for Ellington. There were, however, even greater changes taking place that would affect big band-leaders like Duke Ellington. With the end of World War II public taste was changing again. By the late 1930s, most big bands featured a lead singer. Performers like Frank Sinatra, Dinah Shore, Patti Page, Ella Fitzgerald, and many others began their singing careers this way. Eventually they went off on their own. They didn't need the bands. Clubs and theaters also found that it was cheaper to feature a singer or the small group of musicians more typical of modern jazz, the newest style of music. Then, in the late 1940s, came television. People stayed home more often, and the nightclubs began to disappear. Many movie theaters no longer offered stage shows. There were fewer places for the big bands to play, fewer people who were willing to pay to hear them live or on records. The big bands were fighting for their lives—and losing.

By 1949 Duke's orchestra was no longer making a profit. His payroll was about $4,500 a week, including the salary of his barber, who traveled with the band. But sometimes Duke only took in about $3,000. The band no longer traveled by rail. That ended during World War II when train space was needed for troops. Now the band took a bus from one playing date to another. Duke was paying the big bills to keep the band on the road out of the profits he was making from his songs and from record sales. He felt that he had no choice. The manager of a band that made more money asked Duke why he kept putting his own money into the band. "The band you run has got to please the audience," Duke told him. "The band I run has got to please *me*."

Duke had to keep the band going because it was his artistic tool. He was in a unique situation. Duke needed to hear right away what he had produced. That's the way he worked. That, as he later told a jazz critic, is why he kept "these expensive gentlemen" with him.

By 1950 most of the bands were either gone, reduced in size, or worked together less often. That year the jazz magazine *Downbeat* gave an award to Duke Ellington. The magazine noted that all the other bands it had honored the year before were no longer playing together, including Count Basie's.

Onstage, the Ellington band had lost some of its glamour. The musicians no longer wore the fancy tuxedos that had made them look so elegant. Now they wore suits. Their instruments often looked dull and unpolished. Sometimes when the curtain went up, some of the musicians were late getting to their chairs. They walked on casually, as if no one were looking. A few didn't appear until their solo spot came up. They didn't seem to care.

Duke may have tolerated this because he had no choice. There were fewer musicians around playing

From left to right: Tommy Potter on bass, Charlie "Bird" Parker, Dizzy Gillespie, and John Coltrane.

his kind of music. Many of the best were moving toward bebop, the complex modern, abstract jazz that stressed a dissonant, slightly "sour," sound. It was made popular by alto sax player Charlie Parker and trumpeter Dizzy Gillespie (who briefly played with Ellington). To get and keep good players, Duke may have had to let them behave any way they wished.

But even during these hard times there were limits. One day at a rehearsal, the players seemed to be just going through the motions. Duke usually kept his temper in check but not that day. "Let's go back to letter *E*, gentleman," Duke yelled, calling their attention to the music in front of them, "*E* for Edward, *E* for

Ellington, *E* for elegant." Now he was really hot. "What the _____ do you guys think you're doing anyway? Letter *E, E, E.*"

In 1951 more key players from the old band went their separate ways. Lawrence Brown, Sonny Greer, and Johnny Hodges departed, all to work in a new band led by Hodges. Brown had been quarreling with Duke, and Sonny's drinking had reached the point where Duke was forced to hire a second drummer to back up his old friend on days when he couldn't play. Hodges wanted to be able to play music other than Duke's. These musicians had been at the heart and soul of the Ellington sound. The old guard was all but gone.

During the 1950s, Duke began spending more time on longer pieces. The music world and Duke himself were finally coming to see him as a serious composer. "I am a bandleader and I am a composer," Duke wanted people to know. He hoped to use the band "to win people over to my bigger compositions." If they liked the shorter, popular tunes, they would want to hear his longer pieces, "maybe even enjoy them."

Through 1950, Duke's concert at Carnegie Hall was an annual event. For each concert, he composed a new extended piece. These pieces were "suites," a series of songs, each only three or four minutes in duration— joined by a common mood or theme. Some of these parts, or movements, might feature a singer. Others might be in a dance form. The suites were often loosely held together, the units having just enough in common to be thought of as small parts of a bigger work. The suites had titles like *Perfume Suite, Deep South Suite*, and *Liberian Suite*.

Liberian Suite was typical of the longer works Ellington was composing then. Duke wrote it to honor the one hundredth anniversary of the founding of

Liberia, the African republic formed by freed American slaves. The suite is in six parts. The first is a song called "I Like the Sunrise," which Al Hibbler sang on the stage and on the record. It celebrates a "new day," and it sets the tone of confidence and hope for the new nation. In this section and the five dance movements that follow, the deep, throaty sound of Harry Carney's baritone sax is also featured. There are also growling trombones and a steady drumbeat. The vibraphone solo and a solo for Ray Nance's violin appear on two of the dance sections.

One development that would encourage Ellington to spend more time on these longer pieces was the long-playing record or LP. The LP was introduced in 1948. The old 78-RPM records could hold only one song on each side. These new plastic disks could pack close to thirty minutes of music on each side. This meant one record could hold an entire symphony—or a long jazz work. Listeners didn't have to get up and turn over or change the record every three or four minutes.

Duke's longer works were not well received. Criticism seemed to come from all sides. Some jazz critics felt that he should have stuck with the popular-song format that had brought him fame for two decades. They found the suites too arty, neither true serious music nor real jazz.

On the other hand, others said Duke played too many of the old crowd-pleasers at concerts—tunes like "Sophisticated Lady" and "Mood Indigo." The band had played them hundreds of times before in the same way, said the bored critics. "Look!" Duke responded, "What you see on that stage are fifteen men making a living." The people who paid their way in wanted to hear the old songs. Besides, Duke liked to play both simple and complicated music. "I've always preferred to mix dances and concerts," he said, "to play highbrow stuff in the concert hall . . . and the next night to play a prom."

From the 1930s to the mid-1940s, jazz and American popular music were, for the most part, the same. All of America danced and listened to Duke's music in those years. But by the early 1950s popular ballads sung by people like Perry Como, Eddie Fisher, and Patti Page had pushed jazz aside. Then, in the mid-1950s, popular music began to move in still another direction. It was not one in which Duke Ellington wished to travel. Young people were getting tired of

In the 1950s rock-and-roll became the rage among white teenage audiences.

the sweet romantic music that had replaced the big bands. Urban rhythm and blues began to break out of the inner cities and reach the white teenage audiences. Before long it had combined with other sounds, such as country and western. A new sound was created: rock-and-roll.

Now it seemed that Duke was even farther from "what was happening." His records weren't selling well—a sign that he was losing touch with listeners. There were also fewer good offers for the band to appear in person. His fans had good reason to worry.

In 1955 the one musician whose sound the band probably missed most of all, returned. Johnny Hodges and his alto saxophone had come home. It may have been a sign that things were going to turn around. That year Duke also picked up Sam Woodyard, an excellent drummer. A year later, Duke and his band got their second wind. Once again they would be numbered among America's most important music groups. The incident that brought this about happened in a way that seemed straight out of Hollywood.

In 1956 the Ellington band was hired to play at the Newport Jazz Festival. This was a summer music festival held in a Rhode Island town known for its big old summer homes. At one time Duke might have been the star of the show. But not any more. In fact, he wasn't even given the best spot on the program the night he appeared.

Duke and the band opened the evening's concert, a spot usually given to new groups. Then they left the stage, only to have to return around midnight to close it out. Duke thought he was getting shabby treatment from the promoter. "What are we, the animal act?" he asked. There were about ten thousand people in the audience at the beginning of the evening. By midnight

After the Newport Jazz Festival in 1956, Ellington made the cover of *Time* magazine.

they were starting to drift away. There were perhaps seven thousand left by the time Duke and his men came out to play the final set.

The band featured a piece called *Newport Jazz Festival Suite*, a remake of an old number, "Diminuendo and Crescendo in Blue." The piece made history that night. It called for a solo by tenor saxophonist Paul Gonsalves. Gonsalves, who was known for his bouts with drugs and alcohol, told Duke that he couldn't remember his part in that piece. Duke told him, "I'll bring you in and I'll take you out. That's all you have to do. Just get out there and blow your tail off. You've done it before."

Duke announced the piece to the audience and said that Gonsalves would play a solo between the two parts of the composition. Gonsalves started slowly, playing almost softly against the background of the rhythm section. Then, from the piano, Duke began to urge him on. Also doing some cheerleading was drummer Jo Jones, offstage. He had appeared earlier with another group and now he was hitting the edge of the stage with a rolled-up newspaper, keeping time to the beat.

In the audience, the fans began to buzz. Somebody got up and started to dance. Others followed. People were clapping, and soon they were cheering and stomping their feet. It was as if there was something special in the air. The crowd was going wild.

The only people who did not enjoy it were the police and the promoter. They were afraid that there was going to be a riot. They wanted the concert to end with this piece. But Duke wasn't going to stop now. Not with *that* kind of response from his audience. So the band played four more pieces before they quit.

It's possible that Duke knew just what he was doing that night. Paul Gonsalves's playing sounds very much like the tenor sax solos and rock-and-roll records of the time. Was Duke trying to get the younger fans to listen to his music? We will never know. But one thing is certain. It put Duke back in the spotlight. Several weeks later he was on the cover of *Time* magazine. People were buying his records again and talking about him. And that's the way it would be from then on.

Duke remained a dynamic performer well into his sixties and seventies.

CHAPTER 6

AMERICA'S MOST IMPORTANT JAZZ COMPOSER: *1956-1974*

Duke Ellington was almost sixty. He was still a very handsome, elegant-looking man. The circles under his eyes, which had deepened, seemed to give his face character rather than age. Duke not only looked good, he felt good. Despite complaints from some critics, the public now clearly accepted him as one of the giants of jazz. He was an artist whose fame could no longer be hurt by an off year or two—or by a few bad reviews. His work had become part of America's classical music.

His confidence reflected all this. In the early 1930s he was always a little nervous and uncomfortable when he was interviewed. You could hear it in his voice. Now he was completely at ease with the press, and before the public he was the master. His voice was honey-coated, warm, reassuring. He often joked with his audience, introducing each member of the band and then calling on "the piano player"—himself. By the 1950s he was telling the crowd at each concert, "We love you madly." These words became a kind of trademark for him.

All doors were open to Duke. In 1950 he visited President Harry Truman at the White House, who was known to enjoy playing the piano. The president, Duke recalled, told his bodyguards to take a break, took Duke into his private rooms, shut the door, and spoke to him as "one piano player to another." "After that," according to Duke, "you might have thought we were a couple of cats in a billiard parlor, so informal was our conversation."

In 1963 the band played in London. Prince Philip, husband of Queen Elizabeth, was there. "Why don't we all go back to the palace and put some eggs on," the prince told Duke after the concert. "We can have a jam session." When they got there the queen joined them. Duke really put on the charm, telling her she was even more beautiful than the last time he had seen her. She glowed at his words. Later, Don George, who wrote the words to some of Duke's songs, told him that he was amazed that Duke's way with women even worked with royalty. "It's very simple," Duke told him. "I just tell the Queen of England the same thing you tell little Paula who works down at the pool hall."

By the late 1950s, Ellington was spending even less time with the members of his band when they weren't on stage, at rehearsal, or making a recording, than he had in the early years. They traveled in a bus, but he rode in a car driven by Harry Carney. He also no longer stayed at the same hotel as the other musicians.

Duke had had mixed feelings about many of the members of his band. Some of them had a very rough life-style by his standards. With boyhood pals like Sonny Greer, Duke could look the other way when they overdid it with drinking and carrying on. But this was harder to do with those he met later. Coming from a family that tried to be refined, Duke put a lot of value on being a gentleman. Being proper was important. In his autobiography he praises musician Herbie Jones, who "was neat and clean, neither smoked nor drank. . . ."

By the mid-1960s, some of the band members' behavior was making headlines. Ray Nance and Paul Gonsalves were arrested in Las Vegas on a drug charge, and Nance spent some time in jail. Duke wouldn't denounce people for using drugs. That was not his style. But when someone told him that using drugs would make *him* more creative, he told that person: "It ruins your music. It doesn't make it better. If you want to get high, get high on the sound."

In 1964 Duke made his son Mercer, who now played trumpet in the band, the group's manager. Although Mercer wasn't one of the top musicians and did not take solos, he was good enough to play with his father's orchestra. Mercer also wrote several songs for the band, including "Things Ain't What They Used to Be," which Duke often used to end a concert.

Mercer had grown up calling some of the men he was now asked to boss "uncle." It wasn't easy, he later wrote, managing "people who had led me by the hand to the movies, who had taken me out to the circus, who had bought me candy apples or gone swimming with me."

Nor was it easy for Mercer to be his father's son. "I've always wanted to write scores like Ellington," said Mercer. (He usually spoke of Duke by his last name.) But, as Duke was aware, Mercer wanted just as much to be different from his father. "He's always fought against being little Duke Ellington," Duke said of Mercer in 1965.

Although he stayed at the hotel with the other members of the band, Mercer often ate dinner with his father when they were on the road. But otherwise Duke treated him just like another member of the orchestra. When he introduced him onstage, Duke did not point out that Mercer was his son.

It may say a lot about Duke's attitude toward Mercer that when he wrote about his son in *Music Is My Mistress*, he praised Mercer the most not for his own accomplishments but for championing what was important to his father. "My son, Mercer Ellington, is dedicated to maintaining the luster of his father's image," wrote Duke. "Mercer is always up straight and standing tall in defense of Duke Ellington," he added.

The backdrop for all of Duke Ellington's relationships was life on the road. Traveling remained a basic part of his business. He probably covered about ten million miles in his career. Sometimes the band would play at a nightclub or hotel for a few weeks, but most of the year they were still on the road. Often this meant one-night stands. It was exhausting. Some dance concerts went on for as long as five hours, and the band might play as many as forty-five numbers. After their concert they would pack up their instruments and set off for the next engagement. Sometimes that was as many as six hundred miles away. They might get there at dawn, in time to catch a few hours sleep. Fortunately for Duke, he was a sound sleeper.

Beginning in 1958, Duke and his band often spent part of the year on a foreign trip. That year they went to Europe. In England, Duke wrote "Princess Blue" to honor Princess Margaret. He also wrote *Queen's Suite* for Queen Elizabeth. In 1963, Duke and his orchestra began to travel beyond Europe. Their fame had spread to the point that the U.S. State Department wanted them to go abroad as "Ambassadors of Good Will." The 1963 trip was an eventful one. In India Duke ended up in the hospital with sunstroke. Then the band arrived in Iraq just as rebels were trying to overthrow the government. The band quickly left. When reporters asked Duke what it was like there, he said, "Those cats were swinging, man!"

By 1971 Duke was making his second tour of South America. The same year he also took the band to the Soviet Union for the first time. The United States and the Soviet Union still had many differences. The Cold War was still raging, which meant that very few performers toured there. On his five-week tour of the USSR, Duke was a big hit. The audiences loved his music so much that some of the concerts went on for four hours. They didn't want to let the Ellington band leave the stage. When it was time to go, Duke told them in Russian, "Yavas oujasna lublu." He had learned it just for the trip. It means "We love you madly."

Traveling meant Duke had very little family life. Home was now a large apartment on New York's West End Avenue that he shared with Bea, who did not travel with the band. It was hard for Bea to take Duke's long absences from home. But even harder for her was the fact that when he traveled, Duke was frequently in the company of Fernanda de Castro Monte, an attractive woman who could speak five languages. Although Bea seems to have known that Duke and Fernanda were having a long-term love affair she remained with him for the rest of his life.

No matter what was happening in his personal life, and despite all the traveling, the new works kept coming. Besides more suites, Duke composed his first full-length movie score, *Anatomy of a Murder*, and even wrote the theme for a television show, *The Asphalt Jungle*. Along with his band, but also sometimes just by himself, he joined with the other greats of jazz on many recordings. These included figures in modern jazz, such as Dizzy Gillespie, John Coltrane, Charles Mingus, and Max Roach, as well as singers and musicians who, like Duke, got their start in the 1920s or 1930s. Among them were Louis Armstrong, Coleman Hawkins, Ella Fitzgerald, Count Basie, and Frank Sinatra.

One of the more memorable suites that Duke wrote during this period was *Such Sweet Thunder*, which premiered in 1957. In it he set to music some of the scenes from Shakespeare that he liked. Duke had strong feelings about music and literature that was considered "classic." He thought that too many people feared such works because if they didn't understand them right away they felt stupid. To Duke, the most important thing was first to enjoy a play or a piece of music. You could always pick up the meaning by seeing or hearing it more than once.

In a part of *Such Sweet Thunder* called "The Star-Crossed Lovers," Duke cast Paul Gonsalves's tenor sax as Romeo and Johnny Hodges's alto sax as Juliet. In a number based on the play *A Midsummer Night's Dream*, trumpeter Clark Terry speaks through his instrument one of Shakespeare's most famous lines. If you listen closely to the record, you can hear "What fools these mortals be."

Duke wanted to write music that echoed his feelings about the Far East after his tour there in 1963. But he didn't want it to sound just like everyone else's "oriental" music. Since it would have been so easy to slip into using the sounds that people often associated with the Far East, he waited for several months before he began composing the piece. With Billy Strayhorn, who had remained close throughout all the upheavals in the band, Duke went to work.

Most Western composers use brass to suggest a Far Eastern theme in their music. Duke didn't want this. So he made the brasses in his *Far East Suite* play mostly a backup role. They have a major part in only one section. Instead, it's the reeds—the saxophones and clarinets—along with the rhythm section and Duke's piano, that carry the piece. In one part of the suite Duke's solo has a slightly Eastern sound, but the rhythm behind him is more Latin than anything else.

In his *Latin American Suite*, Duke also stayed away from stale musical ideas. One way he did this was by *not* using the bongo drums that so many others would have put in the score. Duke thus avoided the trap into which many other composers fell. Instead of trying to paint a musical picture of where he had been, he let the lands he had visited inspire him to write in his own style.

Now, as never before, Duke wrote most of his music with a deadline in mind. The piece might be needed for a music festival at which he was going to perform. Or perhaps for a recording date that had to take place on a certain day when the studio was free. Or maybe it was for a stage show, television, or a movie. To some people this sounds less like art and more like just turning out a product like any other business. But Billy Strayhorn once pointed out that even classical composers like Bach usually had to work to meet a deadline. "He wrote a cantata," said Billy, "because he needed it for next Sunday."

Duke was by now more than just famous. He was known and honored worldwide. In 1967 the African nation of Togoland put his picture on a postage

stamp that was part of a series of four showing
famous composers. The other three were Bach,
Beethoven, and Debussy. Duke returned the honor by
writing a suite called *Togo Brava!* It was first performed at the Newport Jazz Festival in 1971.

Many pressures came with Duke's fame. One issue
he was being pressured about was to be more active in
the civil rights movement. He was, after all, so famous
that people would listen to what he said if he spoke
out. Like Duke, the great jazz trumpet player Louis
Armstrong had stayed away from politics. But in
1957, the governor of Arkansas prevented black stu-
dents from going to school with whites in Little Rock.
In doing this he defied a court order. Armstrong was
furious that President Eisenhower did not quickly
force the governor to obey the law, and said so—
publicly.

Duke still felt that his art should speak for him. In
1963 he wrote the music for *My People*, another show
about black Americans and their struggle for freedom.
That same year, comedian and civil-rights activist Dick
Gregory tried to get Duke to appear at the March on
Washington. It was the demonstration at which
Dr. Martin Luther King, Jr., made his "I Have a
Dream" speech. Duke first tried to hold off Gregory
with humor. "I never did care much for walking a
lot," Duke told him. Then more seriously, he added:
"You can do more good for the people if you're the
best at what you're doing and you conduct yourself
admirably."

While Duke admired the courage of those who
actively fought for civil rights in the South, he questioned their good sense. Mississippi was then a dan-
gerous place to fight for equality. Duke said of those
who risked their lives for the cause in that state,
"Those cats are crazy."

Billy Strayhorn, a classically educated composer, collaborated
with Duke Ellington over a twenty-five year relationship.

There was another major problem created by Duke's
fame. Many people expect a star to keep doing whatever it was that made them like the performer in the
first place. But most artists want to keep creating new
things. Now, after so many decades of writing music,
Duke was struggling to find a different sound.

One way Duke could create was to *recreate*. During
these years he made new arrangements for many of
his early compositions. Still, Duke wanted to break
new ground with his music. What could he do that he
hadn't already done? In many of his suites and in
some of his popular songs, he had used elements of
the music of the black church. This is the musical
heritage he now turned to.

It was fitting that Duke turned to religious music.
Since his mother's death in 1935, he had grown more
religious. He began to wear a gold cross around his
neck, say grace before meals, and spend more time

reading the Bible. He even read it in the bathtub. When someone asked him about his education, he replied that he had gotten it in three places—in school, on the street, and from the Bible. But the Bible was the most important. "It taught me to look at a man's insides instead of the outside of his suit," Duke said.

Duke wrote his *First Sacred Concert* for the opening of Grace Cathedral in San Francisco in 1965. He also wrote two more similar works over the next few years. The sacred concerts were mixtures of jazz played without lyrics, choral and solo singing, and spoken parts. In a way they were the substitute for the opera that Duke wanted to write but never got around to doing. They were influenced by the music of the black churches—gospel. In the spoken parts, either one person or a chorus recited poetry based on biblical subjects and passages. The rhythm of the speakers was jazz-based. The first piece of the first concert began where the Bible did. It was called "In the Beginning, God. . . ."

As usual, Duke relied on Billy Strayhorn for help in this major undertaking. When Duke was working on the opening of the *First Sacred Concert*, he asked Billy to also take a shot at it. It began with six notes—one for each syllable of "In the Beginning, God. . . ." Although they were working separately, on four of the six notes Duke and Billy had to choose, they chose the same ones.

Over the next ten years Duke was to give these concerts abroad as well as at many churches in the United States. Duke called this music "the most important thing I've ever done or am ever likely to do." It was his main creative activity in the last decade of his life. Although thousands of people came to these concerts, some critics had serious questions about their quality. James Lincoln Collier called them "something of a mishmash," that was "quite ordinary."

By the mid-1960s, when he was beginning to work on the sacred concerts, the years were beginning to show on Duke Ellington. Many people thought that Duke had retirement on his mind. He seemed to have reached the age when most people slow down. But his composing and performing kept him lively and active. One of his musicians at the time said, "He's found the way to stay young. Watch him some night in the wings. Those bags under his eyes are huge, and he looks beat and kind of lonely. But then we begin to play, he strides out on the stand, the audience turns their faces to him, and the cat is a new man."

Nevertheless, he *was* getting older. And by the early 1970s, he felt an urge to tell his story while he still could. In 1973, Duke published his long-awaited autobiography—*Music Is My Mistress*. In its more than five hundred pages there is much about Duke's life. Most of the book, however, is not a chronological account of events in his life. Instead, there are many short sections devoted to people Duke knew or with whom he worked. Duke tells many interesting stories. But he reveals almost nothing about himself.

Typically, Duke steered clear of controversy. He had to put up with racism throughout his career. Gangsters often tried to horn in on his profits. There were many times when he was at odds with members of his band. Critics sometimes had harsh things to say about the music he had worked hard on and for which he had high hopes. Yet this is almost completely missing from the book.

The person who comes through in *Music Is My Mistress* is the one Duke always presented to the public—a gracious, refined gentleman with a good word for everybody. He was always onstage, never letting any of the private Duke show through. That was the way he was; it was his character. And he maintained the same reserve when asked about his work. He never gave a direct answer when people asked him about how he created his musical masterpieces. Why? He said it would take away the mystery.

Don George, Duke's friend and the man who wrote the lyrics to Duke's "I'm Beginning to See the Light," said that Duke liked to manage his life as if he were directing a show. According to George, "He liked to parade like a peacock. Everything about him was for show and appearance, and theatrics; always theatrics. Life was one big stage and living was a big fairy story and he was Prince Charming throughout the whole thing." George claimed that Duke "could double-talk anybody about anything. He could charm you right out of an argument that you came to give him and make you feel so self-conscious that you apologized to him when you really wanted an apology from him."

Duke's audiences loved him for it. His family loved him, too, although sometimes Duke's personality made that a little hard to do. Duke liked to be in control of things all the time. He tried to run his sister Ruth's life and that of his son. Duke once told Mercer, when his son was thinking of having his own family, "You have the children, I'll take care of them." One of those children, Mercer's son Edward, said that his grandfather was a "conductor." He conducted the lives of those closest to him as much as he conducted his band. Duke knew this about himself, but it was only toward the end of his life, when he was dying, that he could confront it. He wrote then, "I'm easy to please. I just want to have everybody in the palm of my hand."

Duke's few close friendships were very important to him, and now he was beginning to lose these friendships. Death was narrowing Duke's world. Billy Strayhorn worked on Duke's *First Sacred Concert* while a patient in the hospital. He had cancer, and two years later, in 1967, he died. He was only fifty-two years old. Duke was badly shaken. His friendship and musical partnership with Billy went back more than twenty-five years.

Three months after Strayhorn died, Duke and the band recorded an album of his music called . . . *And His Mother Called Him Bill*. The album included some important pieces that Strayhorn wrote for the Ellington orchestra, among them "Rain Check," "After All," "Day Dream," and "Blood Count,"— a piece that reflects Strayhorn's fight with cancer and long periods in the hospital.

In 1970, while at the dentist, Johnny Hodges suffered a fatal heart attack. In 1973, Arthur Logan, Duke's friend and doctor, died mysteriously in a fall. Something went out of Duke when this happened. "It was the first and only time I ever saw him cry," said Mercer Ellington of his father.

When Duke's *Third Sacred Concert* premiered at historic Westminster Abbey in London that year, Duke himself was in decline. He had lung cancer, and he was barely able to conduct his work. In April of 1974 he entered the hospital for the last time. Bea, who was loyal to him through so many years, was not able to take care of him as much as she would have liked to because she was also ill with cancer.

Although he was growing very weak, Duke continued to work from his hospital bed. He asked Mercer to help with the editing of the tapes of the *Third Sacred Concert* so that they would be ready to come out on a record. It was the middle of May. His family did not tell him that Paul Gonsalves, his tenor saxophonist, had just died. On May 24, 1974, Duke Ellington himself passed away. He was seventy-five years old. Only a few months later, Harry Carney, the baritone sax player who had been with Duke longer than anyone else, also died. Bea lived for only a little more than a year. She died in 1976.

In 1969, Duke performed at the White House with jazz great
Willie "the Lion" Smith .

CHAPTER 7

CONCLUSION: A MUSICAL PIONEER

Duke is gone but his music endures. Jazz groups big and small play his work, as do some symphony orchestras. His songs are sung by pop singers, as well as opera singers. At the time of his death Duke Ellington was working on music for choreographer Alvin Ailey. It was called *Three Black Kings* (the Magi, Solomon, and Martin Luther King, Jr.). Its premiere took place in 1976. Mercer Ellington took over the leadership of Duke's band and continued to tour with it for several years.

Duke's greatest legacy, however, was not in the band that he left behind. It may not even be in the more than two thousand compositions he wrote, many of them now jazz standards. Instead, his gift to music

The Ellington funeral in May 1974 was attended by many of the great names in the music business, including Count Basie (*center*).

could ultimately lie in his willingness—in fact, his need, to expand jazz beyond what everyone else thought it was.

Jazz historian Frank Tirro has called Duke a "pioneer" who "scouted new regions of musical space." Duke was never one to accept anyone's rules about how music was "supposed" to be written and played. As the saying goes, he "marched to the beat of a different drummer." This is often at the source of an artist's genius. This is what produces breakthroughs. And this is what gives other artists the courage to push on to even farther frontiers.

Ellington was constantly questioning and searching. He questioned, for instance, whether certain combinations of instruments always had to be used. He heard other combinations, uncommon combinations, and experimented with them. Was it necessary, Duke asked, to rein in the talents of jazz musicians—a very individualistic bunch—in a big band? Did they have to be tightly harnessed in order for the music to sound good? Duke said no. He found the most brilliant spot in a musician's talent and used it, while also allowing the artist to express his or her own individual creativity. Because of this, Ellington's band never sounded tired or even the same.

Finally, Duke helped to propel jazz out of a musical ghetto. Jazz was fine for entertainment, many people thought, but when you wanted serious music, you listened to the classics. That's where you heard extended pieces that were truly "art." Duke Ellington the composer changed all that. After him, such distinctions could no longer be made.

After his death, the music world paid many tributes to Duke. Jazz critic Ralph J. Gleason called him "America's most important composer." One thing has become clear as writers try to sum up Duke's achievements. There is no one category that can contain Duke Ellington. This would have pleased him. In his view:

> it is becoming increasingly difficult to decide where jazz starts or where it stops, where Tin Pan Alley begins and jazz ends, or even where the borderline lies between classical music and jazz. I feel there is no boundary line, and I see no place for one if my feelings tell me a performance is good.

Still, all Duke's music was based on jazz and the blues. Somebody once asked if jazz was serious music. He replied: "No one is as serious about his music as a serious jazz musician."

The Duke returns to where it all started—at a concert in Harlem, 1970.

CHRONOLOGY

1899	Duke is born in Washington, D.C.
1909	National Association for the Advancement of Colored People (NAACP) founded.
1914	Writes first composition, "Soda Fountain Rag."
1915	Ruth Ellington, Duke's sister, is born.
1917	*U.S. enters World War I.*
1918	*World War I ends.* Marries Edna Thompson.
1919	Mercer Ellington, Duke's son, is born. Meets drummer Sonny Greer and helps start The Washingtonians.
1920	Mamie Smith records the first blues record.
1922	First trip to New York.

1923	Comes to New York to stay.
1924	Premiere of George Gershwin's "Rhapsody in Blue."
	Bubber Miley joins the band.
1926	Irving Mills becomes Duke's manager; band makes first recordings.
1927	Recordings of "Creole Love Call," "Black and Tan Fantasy," and "East St. Louis Toodle-oo"; opens at Harlem's Cotton Club.
1928	Johnny Hodges hired.
1930	Composes "Mood Indigo."
1931	Writes *Creole Rhapsody*; Ivie Anderson joins band.
1932	Writes "Sophisticated Lady."
1933	Trip to England.
1934	Tours South.
1935	Death of Duke's mother; he writes "Reminiscing in Tempo."
1936	Writes "Caravan" with Juan Tizol.
1937	Duke's father dies; beginning of relationship with Bea Ellis.
1938	Meets Billy Strayhorn.
1939	Ben Webster and Jimmy Blanton join Duke; band reaches peak.
1941	*U.S. enters World War II.*
	Composes music for the show *Jump for Joy*; Billy Strayhorn writes "Take the 'A' Train."
1943	Premiere of Duke's *Black, Brown and Beige* at his first Carnegie Hall concert.
1945	*World War II ends.*
	Russell Procope joins Duke.
1947	Composes *Liberian Suite*.
1948	LP (Long-playing record) introduced.
1950	Paul Gonsalves joins the band.
1951	Johnny Hodges, Lawrence Brown, and Sonny Greer leave Duke.

1953	Writes "Satin Doll."
1955	Johnny Hodges returns.
1956	Success at Newport Jazz Festival.
1957	Composes *Such Sweet Thunder*.
1958	Duke begins series of annual foreign tours.
1960	Writes *Suite Thursday*.
1963	*March on Washington; President John F. Kennedy is assassinated.*
1964	Mercer Ellington becomes the band's manager; Duke composes his *Far East Suite*.
1965	*Malcolm X is killed.* *First Sacred Concert.*
1967	Death of Billy Strayhorn.
1968	*Rev. Martin Luther King, Jr. is killed; Robert F. Kennedy is killed.* Duke writes *Second Sacred Concert*.
1969	Duke's seventieth birthday.
1971	Tours the Soviet Union.
1973	*The Vietnam War ends.* Publication of Duke's autobiography, *Music Is My Mistress; Third Sacred Concert.*
1974	*President Richard Nixon resigns.* Duke Ellington dies.

GLOSSARY

bandleader The person who directs the musicians in a band

bebop Style of music originated by Dizzy Gillespie and Charlie Parker in the 1940s in which tones were combined to produce a slightly dissonant (sour) sound

blues Black American folk music, expressing powerful feelings, in which the first stanza of lyrics is repeated

chord The combination of three or more tones played at once

concerto A composition for a solo instrument, usually with orchestral accompaniment

Harlem Stride A ragtime piano style in which the left hand plays a bouncy rhythm, almost "walking" across the keys

harmony The structure and relationships of musical chords

improvisation Music that is made up as the musician plays it

jazz Music combining ragtime and the blues in which one or more soloists improvise (compose as they play)

melody A succession of single notes (in contrast to *harmony* which uses chords) in a musical work.

minstrel show Stage entertainment by white performers imitating blacks

mute A rubber and metal device placed in the bell of a trumpet or trombone to vary its sound

orchestral color The use of sound to "paint" a picture or suggest a feeling

piano roll Rolls of paper on which punched holes controlled a mechanism in a special piano that enables it to play by itself when someone pumps its pedal

ragtime Lively piano music in which the left hand plays a steady beat and the right hand plays in a slightly different rhythm

swing Brassy, big band jazz with a driving rhythm

symphonic jazz A long, musically complex work that interweaves different themes

syncopation The effect produced by two contrasting rhythms played together, as in ragtime

Tin Pan Alley A type of popular music first created at the turn of the century; also a geographical area that is a center for composers and publishers of popular music

BIBLIOGRAPHY

Bigard, Barney. *With Louis and the Duke: The Autobiography of a Jazz Clarinetist*. Barry Martyn, ed. New York: Oxford University Press, 1986.

Calloway, Cab and Bryant Rollins. *Of Minnie the Moocher & Me*. New York: Crowell, 1976.

Cerulli, Dom, Burt Korall, and Mort Nasatir, eds. *The Jazz World*. New York: Da Capo Press, 1987.

Collier, James Lincoln. *Duke Ellington*. New York: Oxford University Press, 1987.

Dance, Stanley. *The World of Duke Ellington*. New York: Scribner's, 1970.

Ellington, Edward Kennedy "Duke." *Music Is My Mistress*. Garden City, New York: Doubleday, 1973.

Ellington, Mercer (with Stanley Dance). *Duke Ellington in Person: An Intimate Memoir*. New York: Da Capo Press, 1979.

Gammond, Peter, ed. *Duke Ellington: His Life and Music*. New York: Da Capo Press, 1977 (first published, 1958).

Jewell, Derek. *Duke: A Portrait of Duke Ellington*. New York: Norton, 1977.

Lambert, G.E. *Duke Ellington*. New York: A.S. Barnes, 1961.

Sales, Grover. *Jazz: America's Classical Music*. Englewood Cliffs, N.J.: Prentice-Hall, 1984.

Shapiro, Nat and Nat Hentoff, eds. *Hear Me Talkin' To Ya: The Story of Jazz by the Men Who Made It*. New York: Rinehart and Co., 1955.

Ulanov, Barry. *Duke Ellington*. New York: Da Capo Press, 1975 (first published, 1946).

Williams, Martin. *The Art of Jazz*. New York: Da Capo Press, 1980 (first published, 1959).

MAJOR WORKS

List of Major Works (with date of copyright)

Black and Tan Fantasy	1927
East St. Louis Toodle-oo	1927
Creole Love Call	1927
Mood Indigo	1931
Rockin' in Rhythm	1931
It Don't Mean a Thing If It Ain't Got That Swing	1932
Sophisticated Lady	1933
Solitude	1934
In a Sentimental Mood	1935
Reminiscing in Tempo	1935
Clarinet Lament	1936
Caravan	1937
Diminuendo and Crescendo in Blue	1938
Boy Meets Horn	1938
I Let a Song Go Out of My Heart	1938
Prelude to a Kiss	1938
Something to Live For	1939
Ko-Ko	1939
Harlem Airshaft	1940
In a Mellow Tone	1940
Cotton Tail	1940
I Got It Bad and That Ain't Good	1941
Jump for Joy	1941
What Am I Here For?	1942
Don't Get Around Much Anymore	1942
Do Nothin' Till You Hear from Me	1943
I'm Beginning to See the Light	1944
Creole Rhapsody	1944
I'm Just a Lucky So and So	1945
Black, Brown and Beige	1945
Just Squeeze Me	1946
It Shouldn't Happen to a Dream	1946
Deep South Suite	1947

Liberian Suite	1947
A Tone Parallel to Harlem	1952
Satin Doll	1953
Newport Jazz Festival Suite	1956
A Drum Is a Woman	1956
Such Sweet Thunder	1957
Anatomy of a Murder (movie score)	1959
Nutcracker Suite	1960
Queen's Suite	1960
Paris Blues (movie score)	1961
Suite Thursday	1962
Far East Suite	1964
First Sacred Concert	1965
Latin American Suite	1968
Second Sacred Concert	1968
New Orleans Suite	1971
Goutelas Suite	1971
New York, New York	1972
Togo Brava Suite	1973
Third Sacred Concert	1974

INDEX

money and, 56-57, 64, 68, 73-74, 89-90
musical style of, 9, 15, 29, 32, 37, 43, 50-51, 56, 70, 80, 81, 107-108, 113-115
nickname of, 11-12
orchestra, 15, 18, 32-39, 44-45, 72, 75-76, 80-82, 85, 87-97, 101
parents and, 10-12, 17, 56, 63-64, 67, 72
racism and, 40, 59, 62, 83-84, 106
radio broadcasts by, 43-44
recordings by, 33, 35-36, 38, 54-55, 72, 75, 81, 88, 93, 95, 104
religious influences on, 36, 107-108
singers and, 21-22, 45, 57
theme song of, 36, 78
travel by, 37-38, 59-60, 61-62, 81-83, 90, 100, 102-103, 104-105
women and, 10, 38, 64-65, 73, 100, 103
Ellington, Edna Thompson (wife), 18, 19, 25, 38, 63-64
Ellington, Edward (grandson), 110
Ellington, James Edward (father), 10, 12, 72
Ellington, Mercer (son), 18, 19, 25, 54, 65, 73, 75, 101-102, 110, 111, 113
Ellington, Ruth (sister), 11, 64, 73, 75, 110
"Ellington effect," 51-52
Ellis, Bea "Evie," 73, 103, 111
Europe, James Reese, 13-14

F

Far East Suite, 105
Feather, Leonard, 85
First Sacred Concert, 108, 110
foxtrot, 13

G

gangsters, 28, 37, 40, 42-43, 109
George, Don, 100, 110
Germany, 81, 82, 83
Gershwin, George, 55, 56, 57

Gillespie, Dizzy, 91
Gleason, Ralph, J., 115
Gonsalves, Paul, 88, 96-97, 101, 111
Goodman, Benny, 50, 69-70, 83, 84, 87
Grand Canyon Suite, 55
Grant, Henry, 12
Great Britain, 59-60, 100, 102-103, 111
Great Depression, 68
Greer, Sonny, 18, 21, 27, 57, 59-60, 92, 101
Gregory, Dick, 106
Grofe, Ferde, 55, 56
Guy, Freddie, 29, 55

H

Hall, Adelaide, 36
Hamilton, Jimmy, 88
Hampton, Lionel, 83
Hardwick, Otto "Toby," 15, 17, 18, 21, 32, 88
Harlem, 24, 25, 27, 43, 78, 80, 85
Harlem Stride, 14, 19
harmony, 9
Harper, Leonard, 28
Hawkins, Coleman, 79
Hayden, Palmer, 24
Henderson, Fletcher, 35, 36-37, 45, 51, 68, 69
Hibbler, Al, 93
Hines, Earl, 62
Hodges, Johnny, 45, 48, 75, 92, 95, 104, 111
Hollywood Club, 28, 29. *See also* Kentucky Club
Horne, Lena, 83
hot jazz, 30
Howard Theater, 12
Hughes, Langston, 24, 43

I

"I Let a Song Go Out of My Heart," 75
"In a Sentimental Mood," 70
Irvis, Charlie "Plug," 31

Photo Credits:

Cover, frontispiece, p. 20, Schomburg Center for Research in Black Culture, The New York Public Library, Astor, Lenox and Tilden Foundations; p. 8, 42, 46, 66, Culver Pictures; p. 11, 44, 63, 86, 107, Smithsonian Institution; p. 16, 31, 34, 41, The Bettmann Archive; p. 22, Arthur Johannes/Max A. Polster Collection; 39, 71, 82, 94, UPI/Bettmann Newsphotos; p. 53, Jack Bradley/Frank Driggs Collection; p. 58, Henry Delorval Green/Frank Driggs Collection; p. 96, c 1956 Time Inc.; p. 98, Sygma; p. 112, 114, Associated Press/Wide World Photos; p. 116, NY Daily News Photo.
Color Insert, p. 1, Guy Le Querrec/Magnum Photos; 2(b), 2(t), 3, Frank Driggs Collection; p. 4-5, Martha Swope; p. 6, Ted Rozomalski/Black Star; p. 7, Gary Gershoff/Retna; p. 8, Charles Moore/ Black Star.

Photo Research: Photosearch Inc.